United States
Department
of Agriculture

Forest Service

**Rocky Mountain
Research Station**

Research Paper
RMRS-RP-98

October 2012

Spatial Variability of Wildland Fuel Characteristics in Northern Rocky Mountain Ecosystems

Robert E. Keane, Kathy Gray, Valentina Bacciu

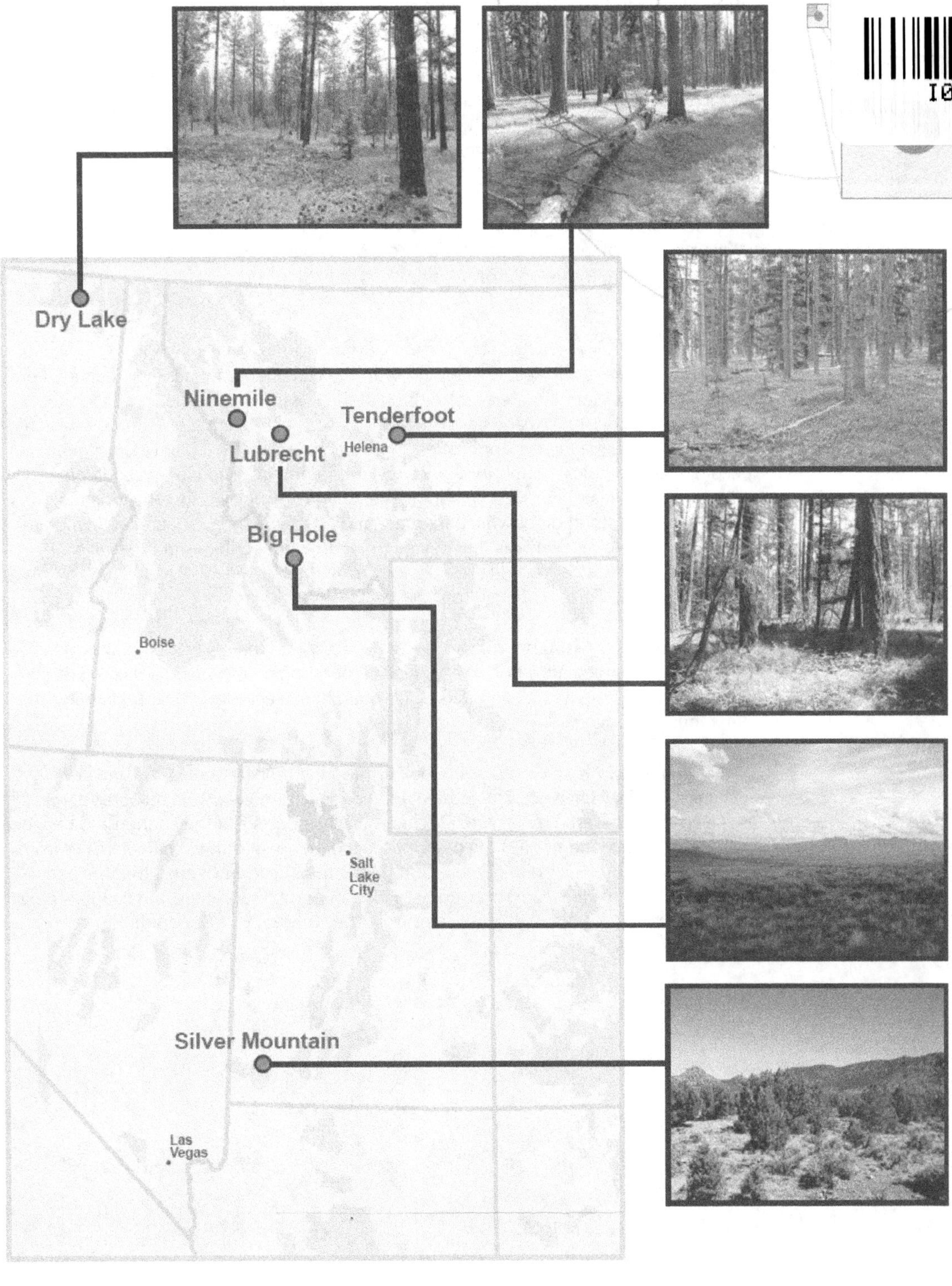

I0435036

Dry Lake

Ninemile

Tenderfoot

Helena

Lubrecht

Big Hole

Boise

Salt
Lake
City

Silver Mountain

Las
Vegas

ABSTRACT

We investigated the spatial variability of a number of wildland fuel characteristics for the major fuel components found in six common northern Rocky Mountain ecosystems. Surface fuel characteristics of loading, particle density, bulk density, and mineral content were measured for eight fuel components—four downed dead woody fuel size classes (1, 10, 100, 1000 hr), duff, litter, shrub, and herb—on nested plots located within sampling grids to describe their variability across spatial scales. We also sampled canopy bulk density, biomass, and cover for each plot in the grid. The spatial distribution and variability of surface and canopy fuel characteristics are described using the variance, spatial autocorrelation, semi-variograms, and Moran's I. We found that all fuels had high variability in loading (two to three times the mean), and this variability increased with the size of fuel particle. We also found that fuel components varied at different scales, with fine fuels varying at scales of 1 to 5 m, coarse fuels at 10 to 150 m, and canopy fuels at 100 to 500 m. Findings and data from this study can be used to sample, describe, and map fuel characteristics, such as loading, at the appropriate spatial scales to accommodate the next generation of fire behavior prediction models.

Keywords: wildland fire, biomass, landscape ecology, woody debris, spatial scale, mineral content, particle density, bulk density, loading

AUTHORS

Robert E. Keane is a Research Ecologist with the U.S. Department of Agriculture, Forest Service, Rocky Mountain Research Station at the Missoula Fire Sciences Laboratory in Montana. Since 1985, Keane has developed various ecological computer models for research and management applications. His recent research includes (1) developing ecological computer models for exploring landscape, fire, and climate dynamics; (2) describing, classifying, and mapping fuel characteristics; (3) investigating the ecology and restoration of whitebark pine; and (4) conducting fundamental wildland fuel science. He received his B.S. degree in Forest Engineering from the University of Maine, his M.S. degree in Forest Ecology from the University of Montana, and his Ph.D. degree in Forest Ecology from the University of Idaho.

Kathy Gray is an Assistant Professor at California State University, Chico. She received her Ph.D in Mathematics from the University of Montana in Missoula. Her research interests are (1) hierarchical modeling, (2) quantitative ecology, (3) sustainability, and (4) climate change.

Valentina Bacciu is a Scientist with the Euro-Mediterranean Center for Climate Change, IAFENT Division, Department of Economic and Woody Plant Ecosystems, University of Sassari. Her research includes (1) the analysis of the relationship between weather/climate and fire, (2) the description and mapping of fuel characteristics from extrinsic and intrinsic point of view, and (3) the investigation of first order fire effect modeling approaches. She received her Ph.D. in Agrometeorology and Ecophysiology of Agricultural and Natural Ecosystems from the University of Sassari, Italy.

ACKNOWLEDGMENTS

We acknowledge Aaron Sparks, Christy Lowney, Signe Leirfallom, Violet Holley, Brian Izbicki, and Greg Cohn, Rocky Mountain Research Station, for countless hours spent sampling, collecting, measuring, and analyzing fuels; and Duncan Lutes and Signe Leirfallom, Rocky Mountain Research Station, for technical reviews.

This work was funded by the National Fire Plan, Rocky Mountain Research Station Fire, Fuels, and Smoke Program, and U.S. Forest Service Fire and Aviation Management.

RESEARCH SUMMARY

Wildland fuel is the one factor that can be directly manipulated to achieve management goals, such as restoring ecosystems, lowering fire intensity, minimizing plant mortality, and reducing erosion. However, many fire managers find it difficult to measure, describe, and map wildland fuels because the great variability of the characteristics of the fuelbed components over space and time makes it difficult to accurately predict fire behavior and effects. Few researchers have quantified this variability over space to understand its effect on fire spread, burning intensity, and ecological effects. In this study, we investigated the spatial variability of a number of fuel characteristics of the major surface and canopy fuel components that comprise northern Rocky Mountain forest and range fuelbeds. Surface fuel characteristics of (1) loading, (2) particle density, (3) bulk density, and (4) mineral content were measured for eight surface fuel components—four downed dead woody fuel size classes (1, 10, 100, 1000 hr), duff plus litter, shrub, and herb—on sampling grids at nested sampling intensities. Canopy bulk density, fuel load, and cover were estimated from measured tree population data to describe canopy fuel variability. We describe the spatial distribution of fuel characteristics along with their variance using spatial autocorrelation, semi-variograms, and Moran's I. We found that most fuel components have high variability (greater than 100 percent of the mean), and this variability increases with the size of fuel particles. We also found that fuel components vary at different scales with smaller fuel particles varying over 1 m scales, large logs varying over 100 m, and canopy fuel attributes varying over 400 m. Findings and data from this study can be used to map fuel characteristics, such as loading, at finer scales to accommodate the next generation of fire behavior prediction models.

CONTENTS

Introduction

Wildland fuel is important to fire managers because, unlike weather, topography, and wind, it is the one factor that can be directly manipulated to achieve management goals, such as restoring ecosystems, lowering fire intensity, reducing fire spread, minimizing plant mortality, and reducing erosion (Graham and others 2004; Ingalsbee 2005; Reinhardt and others 2008). Fuel characteristics are critical inputs into the fire behavior and effects models that are used to plan, prioritize, design, and implement important fuel treatments that could to save lives and property (Andrews 2008; Reinhardt and Keane 1998). Fuelbed information is also used to predict smoke emissions (Ottmar 1983; Hardy and others 1999), quantify carbon pools (Reinhardt and Holsinger 2010), describe wildlife habitat (Bate and others 2004), and evaluate site productivity (Brais and others 2005; Hagan and Grove 1999; Woodall and Nagel 2006). A comprehensive description of surface and canopy fuels is needed for nearly all phases of fire management, including fighting wildfires (Chen and others 2006; Graham and others 2004; Ohlson and others 2006), implementing prescribed burns (Agee and Skinner 2005), describing fire danger (Deeming and others 1977), and predicting fire effects (Ottmar and others 1993; DeBano and others 1998). In summary, effective fire management depends on comprehensive, consistent, and accurate descriptions of the characteristics of wildland fuel that dictate fire behavior and effects.

Many fire managers find it difficult to measure, describe, and map wildland fuels for a number of reasons. Surface fuelbeds consist of a diverse number of components that are often differentiated by the fire behavior and effects modeling objectives (Table 1). A description of fuels for fire behavior prediction, for example, would require the downed dead woody surface fuel loadings to be stratified by particle size classes based on their rate of drying (Fosberg 1970). Fuel components can be specified by size (particle diameter ranges), condition (dead or alive; dry or moist), and material (woody or non-woody; shrub or herbaceous; sound or rotten). And each of these diverse components has different properties that influence fire behavior (Nadler and others 1999; Van Wagtendonk and others 1996). It is this diversity of components and their highly variable properties across space and time that is the main reason fuels are so difficult to describe, measure, and map. The patchy distribution of fuels across a stand or landscape often confounds development of effective measurement protocols, fuel classifications, and spatial fuel data layers suitable for fire management applications at all scales. Fuel loadings, for example, are so highly variable that they often can't be correlated to vegetation characteristics, topographic variables, or climate parameters (Brown and See 1981; Rollins and others 2004; Cary and others 2006).

In natural resource management, the mean or average of an ecosystem characteristic, such as fuel loadings or basal area, is often used to represent that characteristic for large areas such as stands, polygons, or pixels (Keane and others 1998). However, many climatic, biological, and environmental variables are so highly variable across time and space that their mean doesn't fully capture the influence and importance of that variable in the ecosystem. Daily precipitation, for example, is meaningless if it is represented by an average across a year because every day would have light rain. It is both the magnitude and variability of that characteristic that governs impacts on ecosystems, and nowhere is that more evident than in wildland fuels. Fuel properties, such as loading (Brown and See 1981), heat content (Van Wagtendonk and others 1998), specific gravity (Harmon and others 2008), size (Van Wagtendonk and others 1996), and moisture (Agee and

Table 1. Descriptions of the three canopy fuel characteristics and the eight surface fuel components sampled or estimated in this study. We combined the duff and litter layer together in this study because it was difficult to distinguish between the two layers.

General Fuel Type	Fuel Component	Common Name	Size	Description
Canopy Fuels				
Canopy	Aerial fuels >2 m above ground surface	Canopy load (CL)	All dead and live biomass less than 3 mm in diameter	All burnable biomass that is higher than 2 m above ground and small enough to burn in a crown fire (<3 mm diameter) summarized to a per area basis (kg m^{-2})
	Aerial fuels >2 m above ground surface	Canopy Bulk Density (CBD)	All dead and live biomass less than 3 mm in diameter	The maximum bulk density (kg m^{-3}) of burnable canopy biomass across all 1 m layers higher than 2 m
	All material >2 m above ground	Canopy Cover (CC)	All canopy biomass	Vertically projected canopy cover estimated in 10 percent classes
Surface Fuels				
Downed Dead Woody	1 hour woody	Twigs	<1 cm (0.25 inch) diameter	Detached small woody fuel particles on the ground
	10 hour woody	Branches	1-2.5 cm (0.25-1.0 inch) diameter	Detached small woody fuel particles on the ground
	100 hour woody	Large Branches	2.5-7 cm (1-3 inch) diameter	Detached small woody fuel particles on the ground
	1000 hour woody	Logs	7+ cm (3+ inch) diameter	Detached small woody fuel particles on the ground
Shrubs	Shrub	Shrubby	All shrubby material less than 5 cm diameter	All burnable shrubby biomass with branch diameters less than 5 cm
Herbaceous	Herb	Herbs	All sizes	All live and dead grass, forb, and fern biomass
Duff	Duff	Duff	All sizes	Partially decomposed biomass whose origins cannot be determined
Litter	Litter	Litter	All sizes, excluding woody	Freshly fallen, non-woody material that includes leaves, cones, pollen, and cones

others 2002), are astonishingly variable in time and in space, and this variability ultimately influences wildland fire effects and behavior. Fire spread, for example, is greatly influenced by the spatial distribution of fuels (Rocca 2009; Parsons and others 2010); fine-scale patches without fuels can dictate the direction, speed, and intensity of fire spread (Finney 1998b; Agee and others 2000; King and others 2008; Thaxton and Platt 2006). To assign an average of fuel values across large areas, as is frequently done with fire behavior fuel models (Keane and others 2001), ignores the extraordinary influence that fuel variability can have on wildland fire processes. In fire ecology, for example, it is the uneven distribution of fuels across a landscape that primarily dictates post-fire plant mortality, growth, and colonization dynamics (DeBano and others 1998), yet this complex fuel patchwork is often overlooked when managers assume uniform fire behavior.

This research is a comprehensive effort to describe the variability of major fuel properties across eight fuel components on six common forest and rangeland ecosystem types in the northern Rocky Mountains of the United States. We measured these characteristics at staggered sampling points within a large sampling grid to describe their variability across several spatial scales using geostatistical techniques. We also describe the spatial distribution and autocorrelation of these fuel variables. Results from this study may illustrate that many conventional fuel products and analyses ignore scale-dependent variability that may make them inappropriate for future mechanistic fire behavior simulations (Parsons and others 2010).

Background

Wildland fuels

In this paper, wildland fuel comprises all the organic matter available to permit fire ignition and sustain combustion (Albini 1976; Sandberg and others 2001). Specifically, fuel is the live and dead surface and canopy biomass that fosters the spread of wildland fire. Several terms that describe fuel characteristics need to be defined for this paper. *Surface fuel* is the biomass within 2 m vertical of the mineral soil surface, and it is often divided into the *fuel components* of duff and litter, downed and dead woody biomass in a range of diameter classes, and live and dead vegetation (Table 1). It is often difficult to estimate duff and litter loadings separately because it is challenging to assess where the litter (freshly fallen biomass whose origins can be easily determined) ends and the duff (litter that has decomposed so origins cannot be determined) starts. In this study, we grouped both duff and litter together as one fuel component (litter+duff). Downed dead woody fuels are often separated into four diameter size classes based on the drying time of the woody fuel particle (Fosberg 1970) for predicting fire behavior and effects (Table 1), and these size classes are employed in this study. *Canopy fuel* is live and dead aerial biomass that is greater than 2 m above ground and is primarily composed of branches and foliage but also includes arboreal mosses, lichens, dead ladder fuels, and other hanging dead material such as needles and dead branches (Reinhardt and others 2006).

Surface fuels are described by a unique set of characteristics when they are used by fire management to predict fire behavior and effects, and we measured four common characteristics in this study. *Fuel loading* is defined as the mass of a fuel component per unit area, expressed in this study as kg m^{-2}. The density of woody fuel particles (*particle density*, kg m^{-3}) is the mass per unit volume of fuel particles and is a function of the species, particle size, and degree of decay. It is a major factor determining fuel loadings (Brown 1974). *Bulk density* is the amount of fuel per unit volume (Figure 1) and is measured as the mass of a fuel component(s) in the volume of space that defines it in the fuelbed (Brown 1981). This volume is usually estimated as a unit area times the height of the fuelbed or fuel component. Bulk densities of the litter+duff, shrub, and herb fuelbed components are important for estimating fuel loadings (Figure 1) (Lutes and others 2006). *Mineral content* is the amount of fuel component biomass that is inorganic, usually expressed as a proportion, and is important in the prediction of surface fire behavior because high mineral contents dampen fire spread and combustion processes (Rothermel 1972; Hartford 1990).

Canopy fuels are treated differently from surface fuels in wildland fire science (Cruz and others 2003; Burgan and Rothermel 1984). Surface fuels usually accumulate until the decomposition rate equals or becomes greater than the deposition rate (Keane 2008b); while canopy fuels tend to increase as shade-tolerant tree species become established in the understory and then in the overstory (Agee and Huff 1987). Many fire behavior prediction systems do not differentiate among canopy fuel components because of the low resolution of crown fire models (Rothermel

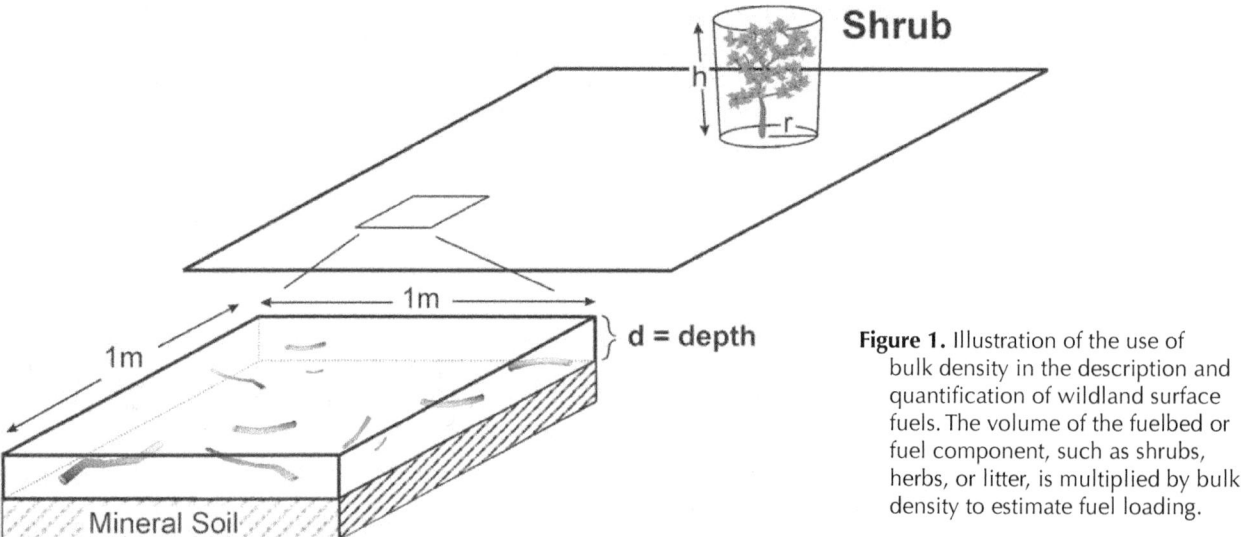

Figure 1. Illustration of the use of bulk density in the description and quantification of wildland surface fuels. The volume of the fuelbed or fuel component, such as shrubs, herbs, or litter, is multiplied by bulk density to estimate fuel loading.

1991) and the minor influence that large canopy fuels have on crown fire behavior (van Wagner 1977; Albini 1999). Therefore, canopy fuels are often described by the biomass that is burned in a crown fire, defined in this study as all canopy material less than 3 mm in diameter (Call and Albini 1997). This amount of material summed over a unit area is called the *canopy fuel loading* (CFL, kg m^{-2}). Since remaining canopy material (particles greater than 3 mm diameter) rarely burns in a wildfire or prescribed fire, it is often ignored in fire management models, yet this material is fundamentally important in carbon dynamics (Finkral and Evans 2008; Reinhardt and Holsinger 2010). *Canopy cover* (CC, percent) is the vertically projected cover of all canopy fuels, including the particles greater than 3 mm diameter. CC is important for describing and modeling the contagion and connectedness of canopy fuels and for the attenuation of solar radiation that drives dead and live fuel moisture dynamics (Anderson 1990).

Another canopy fuel characteristic important in simulating crown fire propagation is *canopy bulk density* (CBD, kg m^{-3}), defined as the mass per unit volume of canopy biomass that would burn in a crown fire (again, foliage and twigs less than 3 mm in diameter; Figure 2) (Alexander 1988; van Wagner 1977). A number of fire behavior and effects models require estimates of CBD and several other canopy fuel characteristics (namely canopy base height, stand height, and canopy cover) to accurately simulate crown fires using models such as FIRETEC (Linn 1997), NEXUS (Scott 1999), and FARSITE (Finney 1998a). Like the other canopy characteristics mentioned above, standardized indirect field methods do not exist for directly sampling and estimating CBD because its measurement requires detailed knowledge of the vertical distribution of crown biomass (Alexander 1988) (Figure 2). Direct methods of destructively sampling tree biomass by vertical canopy layers are prohibitively expensive and time consuming (Gary 1976; Reinhardt and others 2006). The most popular indirect method for estimating CBD involves using measurements of tree diameter, height, and crown base height for all trees in a plot to calculate crown biomass distribution from allometric crown biomass equations (Reinhardt and others 2006). Reinhardt and Crookston (2003) used the Sando and Wick (1972) approach in combination with the Brown (1978) crown equations to estimate CBD from stand inventory data (tree density, species, diameter, tree height, crown base height) in the Forest Vegetation Simulator growth and yield model. Because the vertical distribution of CBD is highly variable in a

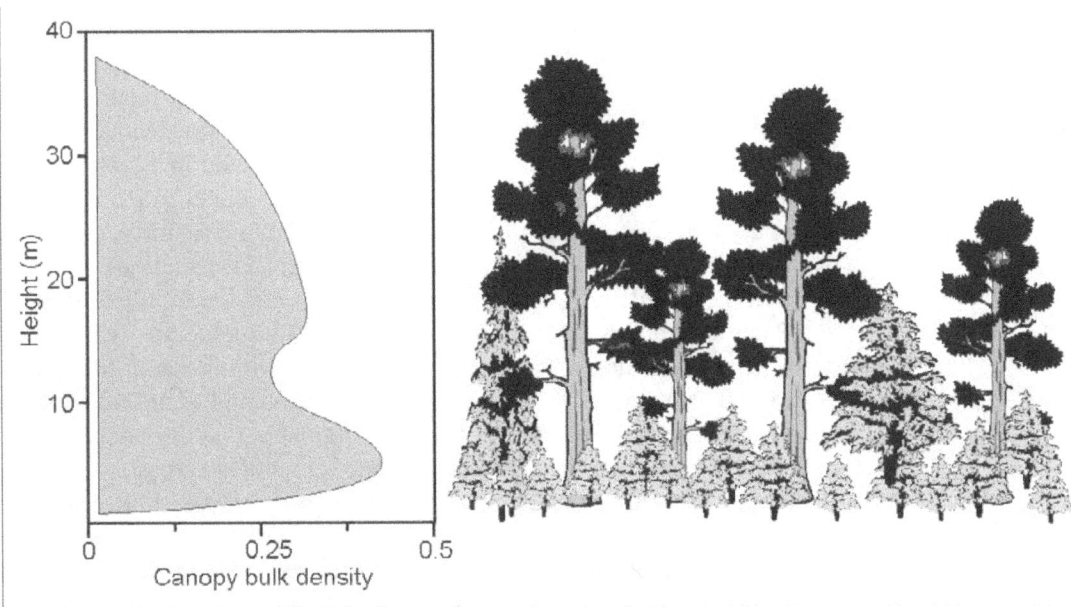

Figure 2. Visual depiction of canopy bulk density and its distribution throughout the canopy profile.

stand, average values across the canopy profile may not adequately represent the fuel conditions required for crown fire propagation (Figure 2). Crown fire spread may depend only on a few dense canopy layers with high CBD. Vertical canopy fuel characteristics are associated with species composition and stand structure where shade-tolerant species tend to occupy the lower canopy and tend to have higher proportions of flammable foliage and fine fuel than shade-intolerant, early seral species (Brown 1978; Roberts and Long 1992). Therefore, any estimate of CBD must describe those canopy layers that account for the majority of crown fire spread.

Fuel Variability

As mentioned, the most notable factor that confounds describing and quantifying fuel is the high variability of fuel characteristics across time and space (Brown and Bevins 1986; Agee and Huff 1987; Keane 2008a). A fuelbed can consist of many fuel components, such as litter, duff, logs, and cones, and the properties of each component, such as loading, mineral content, and moisture, can be highly variable, even within a single fuel particle, such as a needle, twig, and log. And since each component is composed of different sized fuel particles, these properties can vary at different spatial scales (Habeeb and others 2005). The variability of fuel loading, for example, can be as high within a stand as it is across a landscape, and this variability can be different for each component, each fuel size, and each landscape setting (Brown and Bevins 1986; Keane 2008a). It is the distribution and variability of fuel across space that confounds many fire management applications such as fuel classification, mapping, description, and fire behavior prediction.

Assessments of spatial variability have been made for ecophysiological (Rodeghiero and Cescatti 2008), soils (Grunwald and others 2007), weather (Augustine 2010), hydrology (Russo and Bouton 1992), and vegetation (Powell and Hansen 2007) characteristics across landscapes of various extents. However, few studies have assessed spatial variability of wildland fuels. Reich and others (2004) evaluated the coarse-scale (30 m) spatial variability of several fuel components over a large landscape in the Black Hills, United States, by modeling fuel properties from remote sensing products and found that variability was correlated to topography and vegetation. But, they did not evaluate the inherent scale of this variability, or spatial variability at fine scales (<5 m). Hiers and others (2009) measured small-scale variations in surface fuel that were quantified using LIDAR heights and found that heights become spatially independent after small lag distances (0.5 m^2). Parsons and others (2010) simulated fine scale variations in fuel characteristics in a small area using a computer model called FUEL3D, and then input the simulated fuel distributions into highly mechanistic computational fluid dynamics models to simulate fire behavior. Spatial variations of grasslands have been described in the context of population dynamics and restoration potential (Peters and others 2006; Thorhallsdottir 1990). Fuel loadings have been manipulated at fine scales (1 to 5 m) to investigate the influence of fine fuel mosaics on fire intensity and effects (Rocca 2009; Thaxton and Platt 2006). Several studies have described the patterns of fuel distributions across the landscape, but few have actually quantified the variability of fuel properties across space (Jia and others 2006; King and others 2008; Kennedy and others 2008; Miller and Urban 2000). To our knowledge, there have been no studies that assessed the spatial variabilities of multiple fuel properties using field sampling and empirical techniques.

Spatial Analysis

Several statistical techniques and tools were used to describe the variability of wildland fuels in this project. We used the common descriptive statistics of mean, range, and standard deviation to provide context for interpreting the variability of fuel characteristics across a sample site (Sokal and Rohlf 1981; Reich and others 2004). However, the variability is often related to the amount of fuel, so we also included the coefficient of variation defined as the ratio of the standard deviation to the mean converted to a percent (multiplied by 100). We also report *IQR* (*InterQuartile Range* or the distance between the 75th percentile and 25th percentile) and s*kewness* (a measure of asymmetry of a probability distribution). The skewness for the normal distribution is zero; negative values for the skewness indicate that the data are skewed left (many small values, fewer large values), and positive skewness indicates that the data are skewed right (many large values) (Sokal and Rohlf 1981).

Spatial variability is described primarily using semivariograms (Bellehumeur and Legendre 1998; Townsend and Fuhlendorf 2010). The variogram is a descriptive technique that graphically represents the spatial continuity of a data set. The *semivariogram* depicts the spatial autocorrelation of the measured sample points and involves calculating the variance for a pair of observations of a variable as a function of their separation distance (Isaaks and Srivastava 1989). Once each pair of locations is plotted, a model is fit through them. There are certain graphical characteristics that are commonly used to describe these models (Figure 3). Theoretically, the semivariogram value is zero at zero distances, but at small distances, the semivariogram can often exhibit a *nugget* effect, which is a value greater than zero that is often attributed to both measurement errors and spatial sources of variation at distances smaller than the sampling interval (Fortin 1999). Natural phenomena, such as fuel characteristics, can vary spatially over a wide range of scales and variation at distances smaller than the smallest sampling distances will appear as part of the nugget effect. The distance where the model first flattens is known as the *range* (Figure 3). Sample locations separated by distances smaller than the range are spatially autocorrelated, whereas locations farther apart than the range are not. Semivariogram range is important in ecology because it represents the scale at which the entity is best described in space (inherent patch size). The value of the semivariogram model at the range is called the sill or the maximum

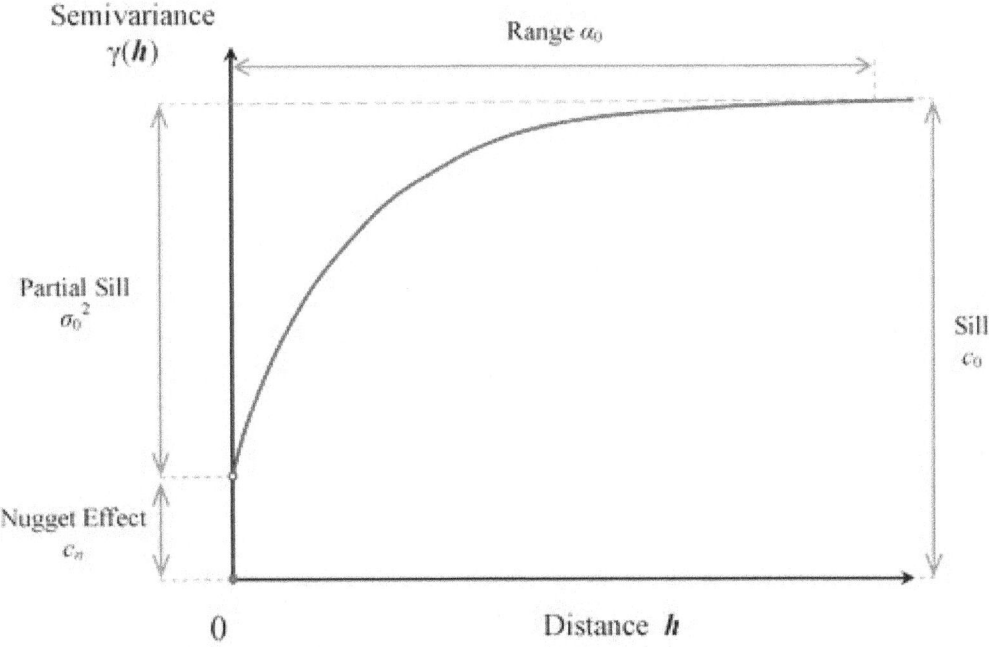

Figure 3. Important characteristics of a semivariogram. The nugget, sill, and range are commonly used to describe the spatial variability of an ecological characteristic.

level of variation in the spatial data (Townsend and Fuhlendorf 2010). This spatial variation can be directionally dependent (*anisotrophic*) or it can be equal in all directions (*isotrophic*).

We also used several statistical indices to describe spatial distribution (Bellehumeur and Legendre 1998). *Moran's I* is a weighted correlation coefficient ranging from -1 to 1 that is used to detect departures from spatial randomness (Moran 1950). Departures from randomness indicate spatial patterns such as clusters. The statistic may identify other kinds of pattern such as geographic trend. Moran's I tests for spatial autocorrelation in geographic data. Positive spatial autocorrelation means that nearby areas have similar values, indicating global spatial clustering, and Moran's I will be large and positive. When rates are dissimilar, Moran's I will be negative. Geary's C is another measure of spatial autocorrelation that is similar but not identical to Moran's I; while Moran's I is a measure of global spatial autocorrelation, Geary's C is more sensitive to local spatial autocorrelation (Cliff and Ord 1970). The value of Geary's C lies between 0 and 2, where values near 1 indicate no spatial autocorrelation.

Objectives

The primary objective of this study was to describe the spatial variability of surface and canopy fuel characteristics for forest and range ecosystems of the northern Rocky Mountains.

Fire managers, carbon scientists, fuel managers, and fire scientists interested in describing and sampling fuels for fire behavior and effects prediction will find this project valuable. This research may lead to new methods of simplifying fuels characteristics to aid fuel quantification efforts, such as fuel sampling, mapping, and classification.

Methods

Sampled Fuel Properties

Even though fuelbeds are incredibly diverse, we only had the time and funding to sample those conventional fuel components described in Table 1, which we considered most important to fire management at this time. Other fuel components, such as needle drape, stumps, squirrel middens, and animal scat (Ottmar and others 2007), were not included because they were (1) rare on the landscape; (2) complicated to measure in a sampling unit compatible to this study; (3) difficult to sample because there were few standardized methods to measure their properties; and (4) unimportant inputs to the fire effects and behavior models. We included most of these special fine fuel components as part of the litter and duff but ignored stumps. In this study, the fuel variables are the four properties for each of the surface fuel components.

Canopy and surface fuels were sampled and calculated differently in this study because of methodological, modeling, logistical, and scale concerns (Reinhardt and others 2006). For canopy fuels, we calculated the biomass of all burnable canopy fuels (dry weight mass in kg of all fuels less than 3 mm diameter) from allometric tree structural relationships summarized into two measurements–canopy fuel loading (CFL, kg m^{-2}) and canopy bulk density (CBD, kg m^{-3}) (Table 1). The third canopy fuel variable, canopy cover (CC, percent), was visually estimated in the field at the plot level. In contrast, surface fuelbeds with their diverse fuel components have many characteristics that are required by fire models, so we sampled the following characteristics for all or some of the eight fuel components in Table 1 or for the entire fuelbed (unless otherwise stated):

- **Loading** (kg m^{-2}). The dry weight biomass per unit area. This was measured for all eight components.
- **Particle Density** (kg m^{-3}). The mass per unit volume of woody fuel particles. We only measured particle densities for the four downed dead woody fuel components.
- **Mineral Content** (proportion). Proportion of biomass that is inorganic. This was only measured for the four downed woody components and the litter+duff.
- **Bulk Density** (kg m^{-3}). The mass of fuel in a unit volume of fuelbed. This was measured for only the litter+depth, shrub, and herb components.

Loading was the only characteristic that was measured at all of the sampling points. The other characteristics were only measured on 20 percent of all sampling points (see next section).

Study Sites

Six study sites were selected for sampling after extensive GIS analysis and field reconnaissance (Figure 4; Table 2). We targeted the most common mature forested and rangeland vegetation types in the northern Rocky Mountains, but these areas had to be (1) homogeneous with respect to vegetation and topography; (2) large with at least 2 km^2 in area to accommodate the large sampling grid; (3) flat with less than 10 percent slope to minimize the influence of slope and topography on woody fuel alignment; and (4) accessible (within 1 km of a road). Few contiguous, homogeneous areas met our criteria, especially in the remote and topographically

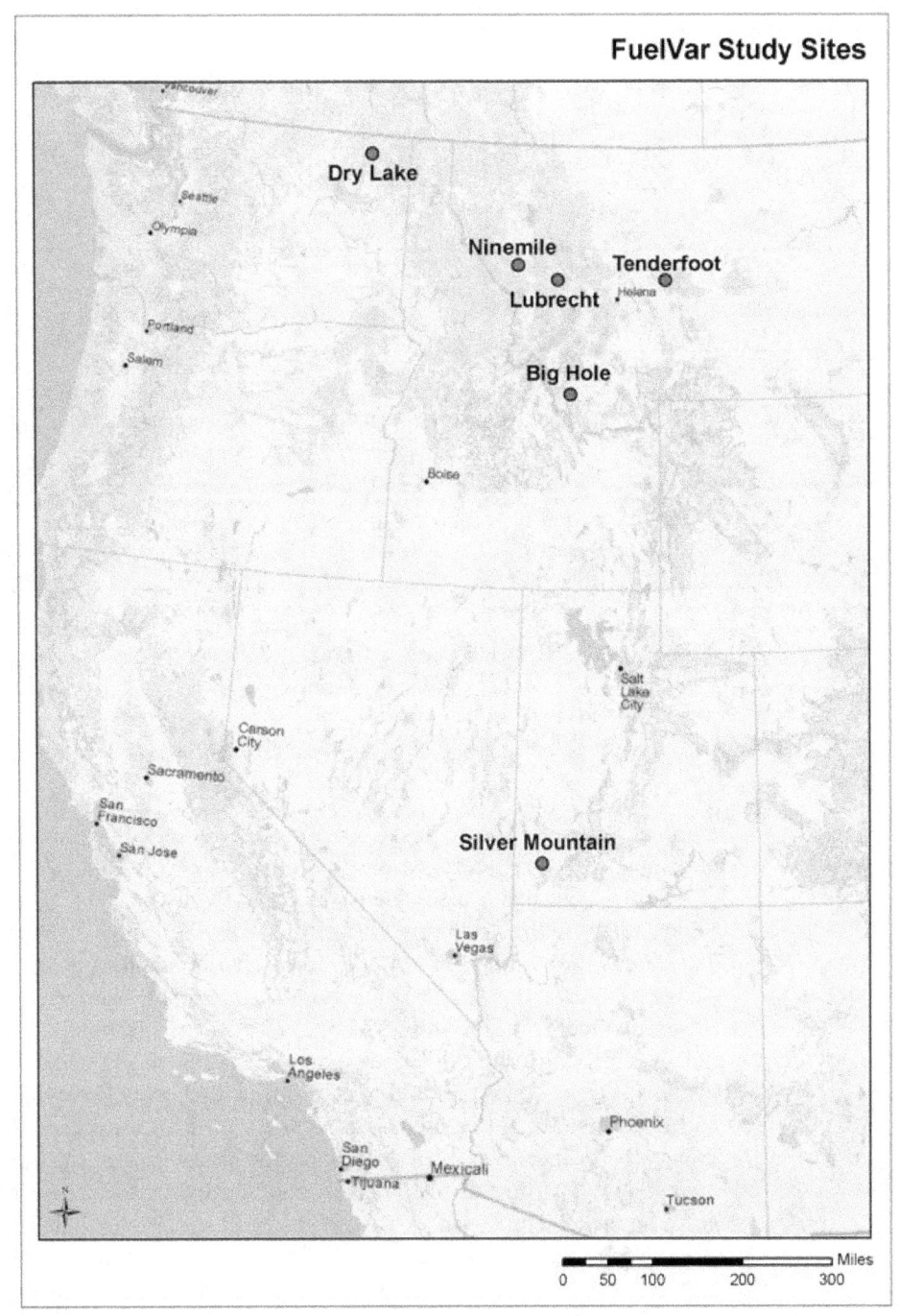

Figure 4. The geographic locations of the six study sites in the northern Rocky Mountains, USA. "Dry Lake" is the Colville Forest site.

Table 2. General description of the selected study sites.

Site Name	Habitat Code	Type[a]	Structural Cover Type	Primary Stage	Dominant Fuels	Past Undergrowth[b]	Activities
Lubrecht Forest	LF	PSME/ VACA, PSME/ VAGL	Ponderosa pine/ Douglas-fir/ western larch	Mature	Partially decomposed light thinning slash	Pinegrass, snowberry, spirea, and elk sedge	Recent thinning nine years prior to sampling
Tenderfoot Forest	TF	ABLA/ VASC	Lodgepole pine	Pole-mature	Low live shrub, scattered woody	Grouse whortleberry, elk sedge, arnica	Low intensity surface fire approximately 64 years prior to sampling
Ninemile	NM	PSME/ PHMA, PSME/ SYAL	Ponderosa pine-Douglas-fir	Mature	Grass, widely scattered thinning slash	Pinegrass, elk sedge, snowberry, kinnikinnick	Thinning and prescribed burn approximately 8 years prior to sampling
Bighole Valley	BV	NA	Sagebrush grasslands	Mature	Sagebrush, grass	Mountain sagebrush, bluebunch wheatgrass,	History of cattle grazing
Silver Mountain	SM	NA	Pinyon pine/ juniper	Mature	Patchy, light herbaceous fuels	Sagebrush, ephedra, poa	History of cattle grazing; wildland fire excluded from these landscapes
Colville Forest	CF	PSME/ SYAL PSME/ VACA	Ponderosa pine savanna	Mature	Grass, scattered woody	Rough fescue, pinegrass, snowberry	History of frequent burning and grazing recent thinning 4 years ago prior to sampling

[a] Habitat types were keyed from Pfister and others (1977), and the codes are: PSME—Douglas-fir (*Pseudotsuga menziesii*), ABLA—subalpine fir (*Abies lasiocarpa*), PHMA—ninebark (*Physocarpus malvaceus*), VASC—grouse whortleberry (*Vaccinium scoparium*), VAGL—blue huckleberry (*Vaccinium globulare*), VACA—dwarf huckleberry (*Vaccinium caespitosum*), and SYAL—snowberry (*Symphoricarpus alba*).

[b] Scientific names are: pinegrass (*Calamgrostis rubescens*), rough fescue (*Festuca scabrella*), kinnikinnick (*Arctostaphylos uva-ursi*), elk sedge (*Carex geyerii*), spirea (*Spirea betulafolia*), mountain sagebrush (*Artemisia tridentata vaseyana*), arnica (*Arnica latifolia*), sagebrush (*Artemisia tridentate*), poa (*Poa secunda* and *bulbosa*), and ephedra (*Ephedra viridis*).

complex high-elevation forests. As a result, we ended up sampling mostly low-elevation, semi-arid ecosystems.

The first site that we sampled was on the University of Montana's Lubrecht State Forest (Lubrecht Forest, LF) in west-central Montana (Figure 5c; Table 2). This site was a second-growth dry mixed conifer stand of ponderosa pine (*Pinus ponderosa*), Douglas-fir (*Pseudotsuga menziesii*), and western larch (*Larix occidentalis*). Overstory trees ranged from 25 to 50 cm DBH and 10 to 25 m tall with the undergrowth primarily pinegrass (*Calamagrostis rubescens*), Oregon grape (*Mahonia repens*), and several species of huckleberry (*Vaccinum* spp.). This site had been thinned approximately nine years prior to sampling, so some residual down woody fuels were still present on the site. Many of our sampling methods were prototyped on this site. The second site was a ponderosa pine-Douglas-fir stand on the Ninemile Ranger District of the Lolo National Forest (Ninemile, NM) (Figure 5d). This site was on a gentle (<10 percent), south-east facing slope in the Douglas-fir/ninebark habitat type (Pfister and others 1977). It consisted of 20 to 50 cm DBH ponderosa pine trees with scattered mature Douglas-fir and sparse Douglas-fir understory. This site had a prescribed burn implemented approximately eight years prior to sampling.

The Tenderfoot Forest (TF) site was on the Tenderfoot Creek Experimental Forest in the Lewis and Clark National Forest in central Montana and is composed of an open, mature lodgepole pine (*Pinus contorta*) overstory (10 to 40 cm DBH trees) in a subalpine fir/grouse whortleberry habitat type with a history of non-lethal surface fires. The fuelbed was primarily low grouse whortleberry (*Vaccinum scoparium*) shrubs with scattered downed woody fuels (Figure 5f). The Silver Mountain (SM) site was an open pinyon pine (*Pinus edulis*) and juniper (*Juniperus*

(a)

Big Hole Valley (BV)
BLM land near Bannack, MT

(b)

Colville Forest (CF)
State land near Colville, WA

(c)

Lubrecht Forest (LF)
Lubrecht Experimental Forest, MT

(d)

Ninemile (NM)
Lolo National Forest, MT

(e)

Silver Mountain (SM)
BLM land near Cedar City, UT

(f)

Tenderfoot Forest (TF)
Tenderfoot Experimental Forest, MT

Figure 5. The six sites selected for this study: (a) Bighole Valley, (b) Colville Forest, (c) Lubrecht Forest, (d) Ninemile, (e) Silver Mountain, and (f) Tenderfoot Forest.

occidentis) woodland with woody scattered fuels, sparse sagebrush shrubs, and frequent depauperate patches dominated by bare soil and gravel (Figure 5c). The Colville Forest (CF) site was a ponderosa pine savanna with a rough fescue (*Festuca scabrella*) undergrowth. Thickets of Douglas-fir trees were scattered in a matrix of widely spaced ponderosa pine trees with DBHs ranging from 25 to 60 cm DBH around 25 m tall (Figure 5b). This site had been thinned in a fuel treatment approximately four years ago to reduce crown fuels by removing Douglas-fir and ponderosa pine sapling and pole thickets. The Bighole Valley (BV) site is a non-forested stand of 30-50% canopy cover of sagebrush (*Artemisia tridentata vaseyana*) with a diverse mixture of grass species (Figure 5a). Because of the lack of trees, no canopy fuels are present on the site.

Field Methods

Sampling Grid Design

We installed a nested grid design within a square 1 km^2 (1000 m by 1000 m) area in the center of each selected study site (Figure 6) (Bellehumeur and Legendre

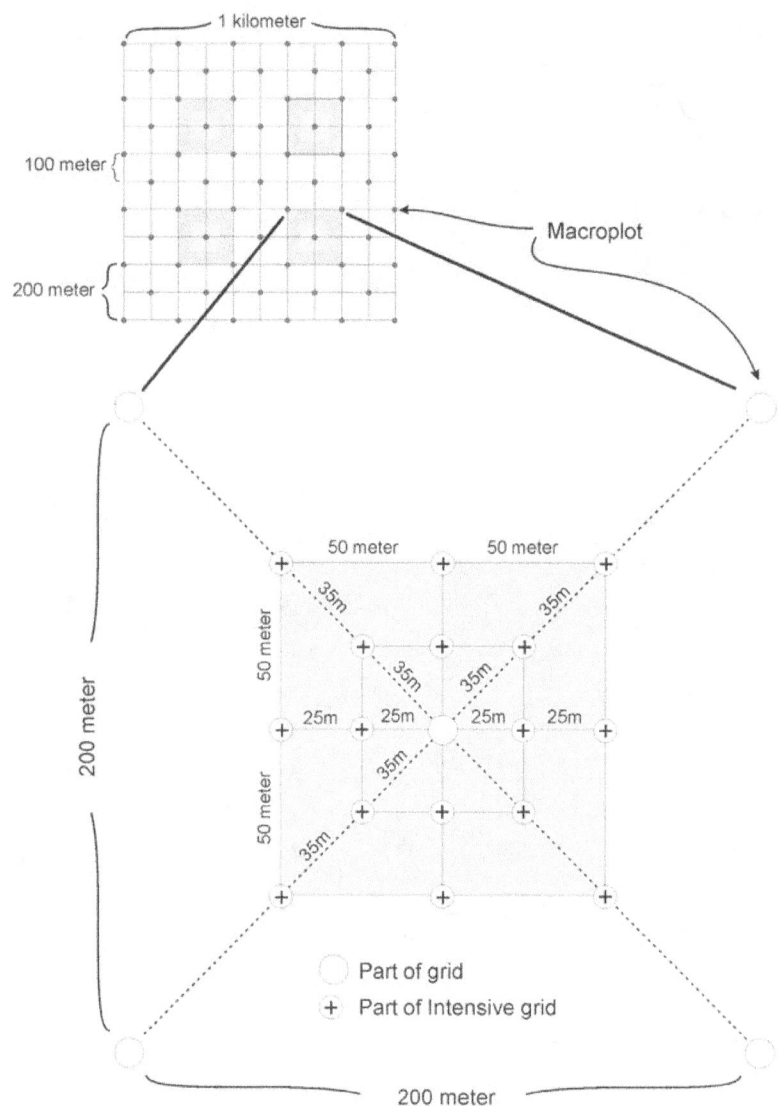

Figure 6. The sample grid installed in the center of each study area with the four areas that received additional sampling to intensify the grid. A set of nested plots were installed at each of the sample points shown in the grid.

1998; McCollum 2005). Corners of this "sampling grid" were monumented using 1-m rebar and georeferenced using a global positioning system (GPS). Sides of the sampling grid were oriented along the four cardinal directions. Transects were established across each corner and at 100-m intervals along each grid side. Transects that were oriented west-to-east were numbered from 00 (NW corner to NE corner), 01 (100 m south of NW corner to 100 m south NE corner), and so on until 10 (SW corner to SE corner). North-south transects had the same naming convention in that 00 was the NW corner to SW corner, 01 was 100 m east of NW corner to 100 m east of NE corner, and so on until 10 (NE corner to SE corner) (Figure 6).

Starting in the NW corner of the sampling grid, we established sampling points at 200-m distances along each of the west-east running transects but staggered the start of the 200-m distance by 100 m on every other transect (Figure 6). Plots along the even transects (00, 02, and so on), for example, had sampling points established every 200 m while plots along the odd transects have plots established at 100-, 300-, 500-, 700-, and 900-m distances. This design provided additional distances between sampling points. Each sampling point was labeled as to its coordinate distance, in hundreds of meters, from the NW corner of the sample grid; sample point 0103, for example, was 100 m south and 300 m east of the NW corner.

We intensified sampling around four grid points to increase the number of distances between sample points. At grid sampling points 0303, 0307, 0703, and 0707 (Figure 6), we installed a nested sampling grid of 16 additional sampling points around a 100-m square (eight sampling points) and 50-m square (another eight points) centered around each of the four grid sampling points. These additional sampling points were placed at the corners and side mid-points for the two nested squares. This intensive grid provided the additional distances, including 25, 35, 50, and 100 m. All intensified grid sample points were again georeferenced with a GPS and temporarily monumented using wooden stakes.

Plot Sampling Design

We established a set of nested plots at each sampling point using the sample grid point as plot center (Table 3; Figure 7). A 400-m^2 circular *macroplot* was established at each sample point for sampling trees greater than 10 cm DBH (diameter breast height) and canopy cover. Using the same sample point as plot center, we installed a 100-m^2 circular *subplot* on which we sampled logs (woody fuel particles greater than 8 cm diameter) and sapling trees (trees greater than 1.37 m tall and less than 10 cm DBH). We then centered a 1-m^2 square *microplot* over the grid sampling point, within which we measured shrub, herb, and fine woody (wood fuel particles less than 8 cm diameter; twigs and branches) fuel characteristics. Last, we installed a 0.25-m^2 (50 by 50 cm) square *nanoplot* in the NW corner of the microplot to measure duff and litter fuels (Figure 7).

Macroplot Measurements

We sampled general site characteristics and canopy fuels on each macroplot (Figure 7) using FIREMON sampling protocols (Lutes and others 2006). First, we estimated general site characteristics, such as slope, elevation, and aspect, using FIREMON Plot Description methods and plot forms (Lutes and others 2006). These general site characteristics provided context and categories for data stratification and pooling. Other important visually estimated data were tree, shrub, and herbaceous canopy cover; ground cover; fire behavior fuel model; and most importantly, CC (percent). We also took several photos of each sample point to visually describe the biological conditions (Figure 5).

Table 3. Summary of the wildland fuel components sampled in this study and the scale and method at which they are sampled.

Fuel Component	Sample Unit and Size	Sub-Sampled?	Sub-Sampling Frequency[a]	Sampling Method[b]
Surface Fuels				
1 hour woody	Microplot 1 m^2	Yes	Every 5 micro	Photoload; collection; length measurements
10 hour woody	Microplot 1 m^2	Yes	Every 5 micro	Photoload; collection; length measurements
100 hour woody	Microplot 1 m^2	Yes	Every 5 micro	Photoload; collection; length measurements
1000 hour woody	Subplot 100 m^2	No	Not needed	Diameters-length, rot class
Shrub	Microplot 1 m^2	Yes	Every 5 micro	Photoload; collection; cover-height
Herb	Microplot 1 m^2	Yes	Every 5 micro	Photoload; collection; cover-height
Litter+Duff	Nanoplot 0.25 m^2	Yes	Every 5 micro	FIREMON depth
Canopy Fuels				
Canopy fuel via tree population allometric relationships	Macroplot 400 m^2	No	Not needed	Tree DBH, height, crown base height

[a]Sub-sampling was used to destructively collected all fuel within the microplot and bring to the laboratory to dry and weigh. These sub-sampled weights were correlated to photoload estimates to correct photoload estimates.

[b]Methods used in this study include the FIREMON Tree Data (TD) survey as detailed in Lutes and others (2006), Photoload fuel loading visual estimates detailed in Keane and Dickenson (2007), the length method involves measuring the total length of the fuel particles in the sampling unit as detailed by Sikkink and Keane (2008), and the FIREMON depth method where depth is multiplied by a bulk density to estimate loading (Lutes and others 2006).

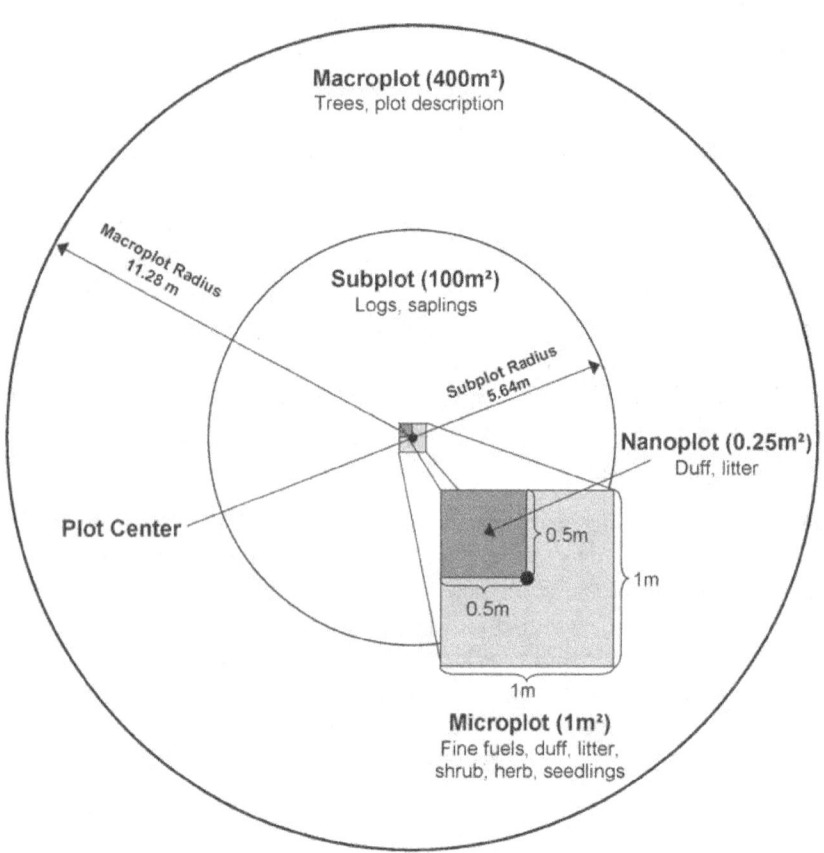

Figure 7. The nested plots that were established at each of the sampling points. The circular macroplot was a 400 m^2, the circular subplot was 100 m^2, the square microplot was 1 m^2, and the square nanoplot was 0.25 m^2. All plots but the nanoplot used the grid sampling point as plot center.

We then recorded tree population data using the FIREMON Tree Data method for all trees larger than saplings within the macroplot (Table 3). Tree population data were used as input to allometric biomass equations to calculate the CBD and CFL canopy fuels variables (Reinhardt and others 2006). We recorded species and health class for all trees above 10 cm DBH and then measured their DBH (cm), tree height (m), canopy fuel base height (m), crown class, crown position, and live crown ratio. Tree crown height and base were measured using a hypsometer or clinometer. We measured the trees in order from the north progressing clockwise around the plot.

Subplot Measurements

We measured all saplings (trees less than 10 cm DBH and greater than 1.37 m in height) within a circular 100-m^2 subplot (Figure 7) again using the FIREMON methods. Saplings were individually measured for species, DBH class (2 cm), height, and crown base height (Table 3). These sapling measurements were augmented with the larger tree measurements to compute canopy fuel variables.

Three dimensions of all downed dead woody fuel particles greater than 8 cm diameter (logs) were also measured within the 100-m^2 subplot using cloth tapes and rulers. We measured the small and large end log diameters and the length of each log within subplot boundaries and then assessed the log's decay class using the five rot classes described in the FIREMON Fuel Loading method. A log's length was measured along the longitudinal axis and terminated at the boundary of the circular plot. Only logs whose central longitudinal axis was above the litter-duff surface were measured. From a 10 percent sample of measured logs, we took at least three cross-sectional areas from selected logs within the subplot to measure log particle densities. Sub-sampled logs were selected for species and rot class. Log cross-sections were placed in labeled paper bags and transported back to the lab where they were dried and weighed to determine particle density.

Microplot Measurements

Seedlings (trees less than 1.37 m in height) were counted by species and height classes on square 1-m^2 microplots (Figure 7) using the FIREMON Tree Data methods. We then estimated vertically projected canopy cover (percent) and average height (m) of each vascular plant species within the microplot using the Cover Frequency method in FIREMON. Fuel loadings for each of the 1 hr, 10 hr, 100 hr, shrub, and herb fuel components were visually estimated using the photoload technique (Keane and Dickinson 2007b). We also visually estimated the ground cover of rock, soil, wood, litter+duff, and moss. Last, we inserted a ruler downward through the duff and litter layers until we hit mineral soil, then read the total litter+duff depth directly from the ruler at 13 points within the microplot (Figure 8) using FIREMON Fuel Loading methods. Microplot measurements were always the first conducted on the sample point so the fragile fuelbed wouldn't be disturbed from trampling.

An intensive microplot grid was installed at the four sampling points that were used to intensify the microplot sampling grid to increase the number of fine scale distances (Figure 9). At the plot centers of points 0303, 0307, 0703, and 0707, we installed a 5-m by 5-m grid containing 25 microplots. The center of the microplot grid was the sampling grid point and macroplot center. All four corners of the 5-m grid area were located using a 20-cm nail. Cloth tapes were tightly attached to each corner nail to guide the sampling of the 25 microplots. All 25 microplots in the intensive microplot grid were measured exactly the same as the other microplots on the 1-km^2 sampling grid.

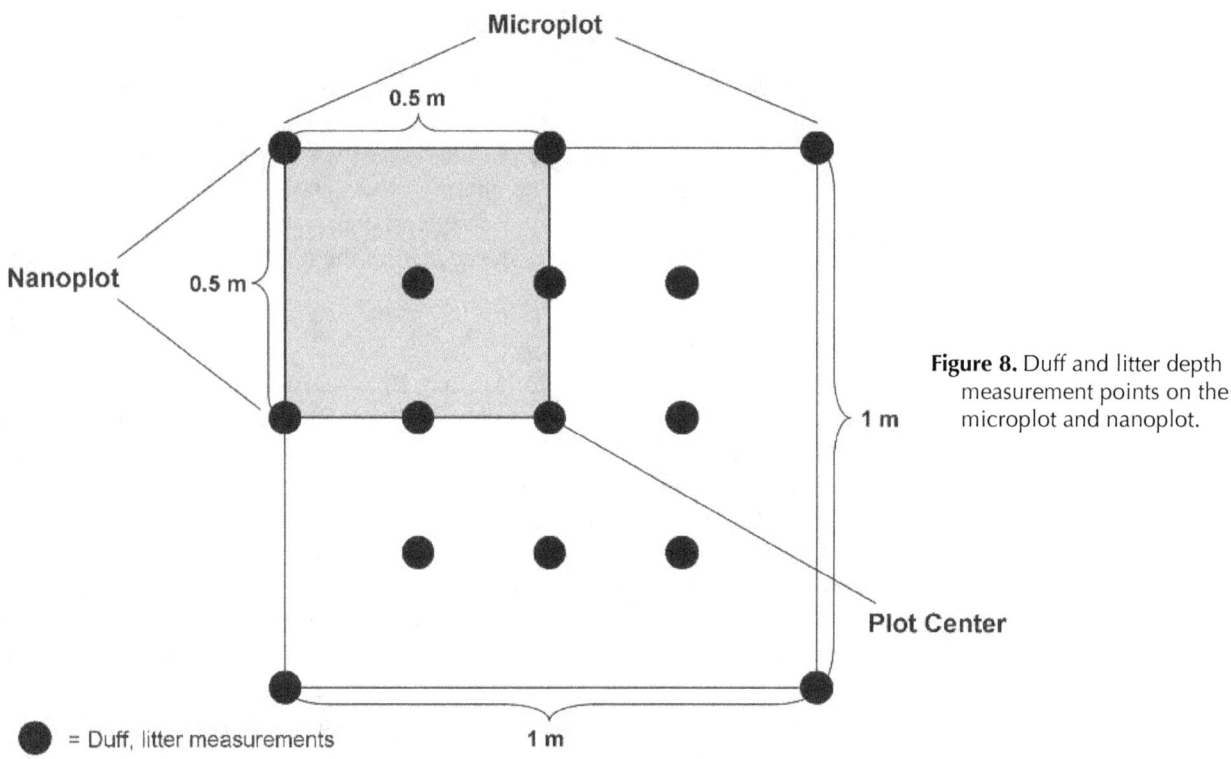

Figure 8. Duff and litter depth measurement points on the microplot and nanoplot.

Intensive Sampling Grid

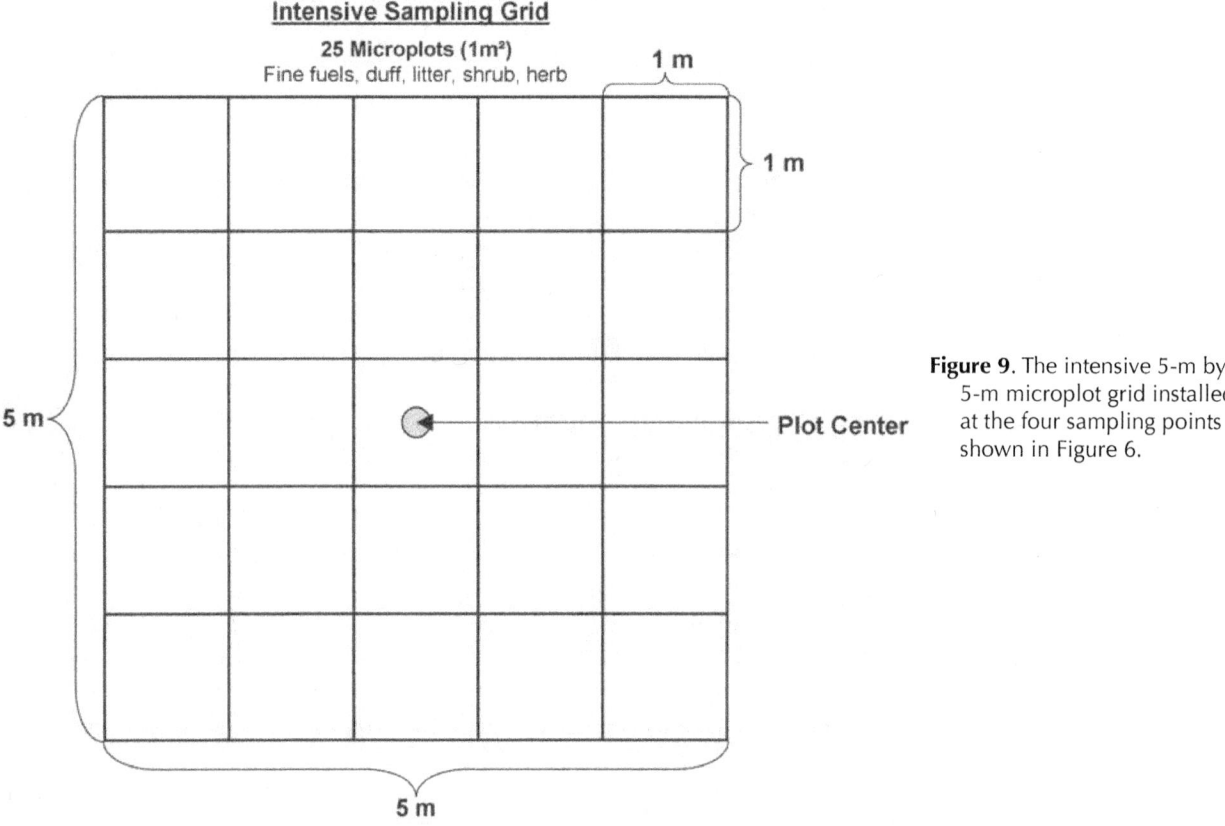

Figure 9. The intensive 5-m by 5-m microplot grid installed at the four sampling points shown in Figure 6.

We randomly selected 20 percent of the microplots, including those on the intensive microplot grid, to destructively sample all fuel for the measurement of actual fuel loading to calibrate and adjust the photoload visual estimates (Table 3). Once the photoload estimates were taken, the total lengths of all woody particles within each of the three fine woody components were measured using a cloth tape on these randomly selected microplots. Length was used to calculate volume, and volume multiplied by wood density provided a more accurate estimate of loading (Sikkink and Keane 2008). We then collected all the fuel in 1, 10, 100, shrub, and herb components and sorted them on site into separate paper bags. These bags were labeled and placed in a burlap bag for transport to the lab where they were dried and weighed to determine loading.

Nanoplot Measurements

One nanoplot (50 cm by 50 cm; Figure 7) was established in the NW corner of each microplot to estimate duff-litter loadings. We measured litter+duff depths for seven points at each corner of the nanoplot and directly in the middle (Figure 8). Duff and litter depths were taken using FIREMON procedures where depth of the entire duff-litter profile was taken (we did not estimate duff and liter depth separately). Litter+duff depth was measured from the top of the mineral soil to the top of the litter material at each point of measurement. This did not include grass, forbs, and shrub height—only the height to the top of the downed dead woody fuels on the forest floor. The five microplot litter+duff measurements, plus an additional two depth measurements (NE and SW corners of the nanoplot), were used to compute litter+duff volume (see next section).

We collected all duff and litter material from the nanoplots on the 20 percent randomly selected, destructively sampled microplots using a flat shovel, trowel, and soil knife. The extracted profile was then stored in a labeled burlap or paper bag (Snell 1979; Stephens and others 2004) and brought to the laboratory where profile was dried and weighed to determine loading. This loading was then converted to litter+duff bulk density using the depth measurements, and the calculated bulk densities were used to calculate duff and litter loading for all the remaining microplots. Only the nanoplot on the center microplot within the intensive 5 by 5-m microplot grid was sampled for litter+duff bulk density.

Laboratory Measurements

All collected fuels that were brought to the laboratory for additional measurements were first measured for dry weight by weighing the fuel after it had been dried in an oven for three days at 80 °C . Dry weights were measured for all collected fuel particles, log cross sections, and litter+duff profiles.

All collected fine woody fuel particles were measured to determine particle volume. We measured the end diameter of the particle, then moved over the particle to determine when the diameter changed by more than 2 mm. The distance from the end to this point was measured to the nearest mm, and both the distance and second diameter were recorded. This process was repeated until the end of the particle was encountered; at that point, we measured the distance and other end point diameter. We calculated the interval particle volume using the particle's length and small and large diameter measurements assuming a truncated frustum shape. Results from this sampling and measurement are not discussed in this report but were used to estimate volume of fuel particles.

Particle densities for downed woody fuel were then calculated from the dry weights and volume of each woody particle gathered from the sub-sampled microplots (fine woody fuel components) and the sawn log cross-sections (coarse woody fuel component). We estimated a volume by immersing the particle in water and recording its displacement (Fasth and others 2010). We coated the smaller particles with wax or paraffin to reduce water absorption into the wood. We randomly selected at most three particles for each fuel component from each microplot. For unsampled woody species, we used density values from the literature (Green and others 1999; Harmon and others 2008; Nalder and others 1999) to estimate loading.

An assessment of mineral content of the fuelbed is important because high mineral concentrations can influence fire behavior by dampen fire spread and intensity (Rothermel 1972). We measured mineral content by grinding a pre-weighed portion of the collected dried fuel from each fuel component in the microplot subsample and burning that ground portion in a muffle furnace for 24 hours and then weighing the ash.

Analysis

We calculated the variability of a total of 22 fuel variables—19 surface fuel variables that describe the four major characteristics of the eight surface components, and 3 canopy fuel variables (CC, CBD, CFL) estimated from the tree population data that describe the major canopy fuel characteristics (Table 4). The values of these 22 fuel variables were either estimated from direct measurements

Table 4. List of fuel variables that are used to describe the variability of major fuel characteristics in the northern Rocky Mountains. Note that some characteristics are only for specific fuel components.

Fuel Characteristic	Fuel Component	Fuel Variable Name	Description
		Surface Fuels	
Loading $(kg\ m^{-2})$	1 hour woody	L1	Biomass per unit area of downed dead woody twigs
	10 hour woody	L10	Biomass per unit area of downed dead woody branches
	100 hour woody	L100	Biomass per unit area of downed dead woody large branches
	1000 hour woody	L1000	Biomass per unit area of downed dead woody logs
	Shrub	LSHRUB	Live and dead biomass per unit area of shrubs
	Herb	LHERB	Live and dead biomass per unit area of shrubs
	Litter+Duff	LDUFF	Biomass per unit area of duff and litter
Particle density $(kg\ m^{-3})$	1 hour woody	PD1	Density of downed dead woody twigs
	10 hour woody	PD10	Density of downed dead woody branches
	100 hour woody	PD100	Density of downed dead woody large branches
	1000 hour woody	PD1000	Density of downed dead woody logs
Bulk density $(kg\ m^{-3})$	Shrub	BDSHRUB	Bulk density of live and dead shrub layer
	Herb	BDHERB	Bulk density of live and dead herb layer
	Duff+Litter	BDLDUFF	Bulk density of the litter and duff layer
Mineral content (%)	1 hour woody	MC1	Mineral content of downed dead woody twigs
	10 hour woody	MC10	Mineral content of downed dead woody branches
	100 hour woody	MC100	Mineral content of downed dead woody large branches
	1000 hour woody	MC1000	Mineral content of downed dead woody logs
	Duff+Litter	MCDUFFLIT	Mineral content of downed dead woody duff and litter
		Canopy Fuels	
Canopy fuel loading $(kg\ m^{-2})$	Canopy fuels	CFL	Biomass per unit area of the burnable crown fuel
Canopy bulk density $(kg\ m^{-3})$	Canopy fuels	CBD	Maximum bulk density of the canopy for the burnable crown fuel
Canopy cover (%)	Canopy fuels	CC	Vertically projected canopy cover of the canopy fuels

made in the field or computed from the field sampled measurements. This section describes the computations used to calculate those fuel variable values not directly measured in the field.

Calculating Surface Fuel Loading Variables

As mentioned, we measured fuel loading from all microplots using two methods in a double sampling technique (Okafor and Lee 2000). Fine fuel loadings (1, 10, 100 hr size classes) were estimated on all microplots using the visual photoload sampling technique because it was easy, fast, and somewhat accurate (Sikkink and Keane 2008). However, photoload loading estimates are based on visual assessments, which may be of sufficient resolution for management applications but probably should be further refined for research measurements. Therefore, we used a regression approach to correlate the destructively collected and measured fine fuel loadings to the photoload fuel estimates to improve microplot loading estimations. We regressed photoload visual estimates for the fine woody, shrub, and herb fuels to the destructively sampled loading estimates for the 20 percent sub-sample of the microplots. The regression equation was applied to the photoload estimates to "correct" the loading estimates for all microplots. The coefficients of determination (R^2) and correction factors for the fine fuel loadings are shown in Table 5.

Log loadings on the subplot were calculated by summing the mass of all measured logs on the subplot and dividing by 100 (area of subplot, m^2) to convert to kg m^{-2} units. Biomass of individual logs (m, g) was calculated by multiplying log volume by the measured wood density using the following equation:

$$M=VD \qquad (1)$$

where V is the volume of the particle (m^3), and D is the wood density (kg m^{-3}) quantified from laboratory analysis of the collected woody fuel (see previous section). Particle volume (V, M^3) was calculated using the following equation:

$$v = \frac{l}{3}\left[(a_s + a_l) + \sqrt{(a_s a_l)}\right] \qquad (2)$$

Table 5. Statistics for the photoload-actual fuel regression equations that were used to adjust visual fuel loading estimates to calculate the fuel loading values at each sampling point used in the study.

Fuel Component	Lubrecht (LF)	Tenderfoot (TF)	Ninemile (NM)	Bighole (BV)	Silver (SM)	Colville (CF)
Coefficient of Determination (R^2)						
1 hour	0.825	0.677	0.765	0.424	0.518	0.494
10 hour	0.573	0.595	0.661	0.420	0.735	0.509
100 hour	*	***	0.777	***	***	*
Shrub	**0.761	0.757	0.510	0.262	0.706	0.415
Herb	0.287	*	0.265	*	*	0.471
Correction Factor (intercept, slope)						
1 hour	-0.0007, 0.500	-0.009, 0.843	0.001, 0.431	0.002, 0.127	-3.03, 0.578**	0.009, 0.167
10 hour	-0.012, 5.480	-0.012, 3.528	0.462, 0.991**	0.003, 0.702	-0.002, 0.936	0.029, 0.614
100 hour	*	***	0.173, 0.881	***	***	*
Shrub	-0.100, 0.926**	0.100, 1.20****	0.016, 1.46	0.169, 0.364	0.000, 0.401	0.019, 1.150
Herb	0.017, 0.289	*	0.020, 0.501	*	*	0.025, 0.693

*Model Insignificant and did not improve visual estimates

**Natural log transformation on both visual and measured observations

***Too few values to build a model; visual estimates were used

****Log base 10 transformation on both visual and measured observations

where a and a_l are the areas (m^2) of the small and large end of the fuel particle ($a = \pi d^2/4$, where d is the log diameter, m), respectively, and l is the length of the particle (m). We assumed particle shape approximated a truncated frustum. Wood density (kg m^{-3}) was directly calculated from all samples taken by species and rot class from the site for all sizes of woody fuel particles (see previous section). If a species or rot class density was un-sampled, we used values taken from the literature. To determine densities, we divided the total mass of the collected fuel particles for a size class by the total volume as calculated from equation (2).

Loading (L, kg m^{-2}) for the litter+duff was calculated by multiplying the volume of the litter+duff layer (V, m^3) by bulk density using a variation of equation (1):

$$L = \frac{(V)(BD)}{A} \tag{3}$$

where BD is the litter+duff bulk density (kg m^{-3}) (Snell 1979; Stephens and others 2004; Woodard and Martin 1980) and A is the area (m^2) of the microplot sampling frame (1 m^2). The volume was calculated using the following equation:

$$V = dA \tag{4}$$

where d is the average depth (m) of all 13 litter+duff depth measurements taken on the microplot and A is the area of the microplot (1 m^2). The BD for litter+duff is an average of all bulk densities calculated from the destructively collected nanoplot samples removed from the 20 percent microplot subsample. To compute field-sampled duff and litter bulk densities, we first computed the loading by dividing the dry weight of the litter and duff profile by the nanoplot area (0.25 m^2). We then divided this loading by the measured volume of the nanoplot duff-litter profile. The volume was computed using equation (4) where d was the average of the five nanoplot depth measurements, and A was the nanoplot area.

Calculating Canopy Fuel Variables

CFL and CBD were computed using the FUELCALC program. FUELCALC was initially developed for the LANDFIRE program (Keane and others 2006) and was refined by Scott and others (2011). FUELCALC computes several canopy fuel characteristics based on allometric equations relating individual tree size, canopy, and species characteristics to crown biomass. The canopy characteristics for a stand are computed from a tree list that specifies the tree species, density (trees per unit area), DBH, height, crown base height, and crown class. CFL is computed by dividing the sum of all burnable canopy biomass (particles less than 3 mm diameter) by the area of the plot within which the trees were sampled (400 m^2 for this study). FUELCALC was then used to compute vertical canopy fuel distribution using the Reinhardt and others (2006) algorithms that evenly distribute crown biomass over the live crown for each tree and divide the canopy fuel summed across all trees into horizontal layers of a user-specified width and reports the CBD value of the layer with the greatest CBD (see Figure 2).

CC (percent) was visually estimated in the field using the FIREMON methods where percent vertically projected canopy cover for all trees greater than 2 m tall was recorded on the Plot Description form using the FIREMON cover classes (0, 1, 3 = 1-5 percent, 10 = 5-15 percent, and so on).

Table 6. Site variables used to correlate with the surface and canopy fuel variables to explain the sources of variation in fuel distributions.

Variable Name	Description	Source	Units
AVEDBH	Average DBH (quadratic mean)	FIREMON Tree Data	cm
AVEHT	Average tree height	FIREMON Tree Data	m
BAREA	Overstory basal area	FIREMON Tree Data	$m^2 \, ha^{-1}$
TDENSITY	Trees per hectare	FIREMON Tree Data	$m^2 \, ha^{-1}$

Calculating Fuel Variability

We first calculated the descriptive statistics of mean, standard deviation, range, coefficient of variation, skewness, and IQR for all 22 fuel variables. We then compared and contrasted these variables across ecosystem types (study sites) using standard statistical tests. Relationships of the variance across fuel components and particle size were then explored using graphical and regression techniques, and tests for equal variance were conducted (Levene's test). Next, we used correlation analysis to evaluate if any of the commonly used stand variables shown in Table 6 explained any of the variance in fuel variables, and also if the surface and canopy fuel components were related.

The spatial variation of surface fuel variables was described using the spatial statistical analysis techniques described in the Introduction. First, we used spatial autocorrelation analysis to construct semivariograms for each fuel variable to determine the scale at which that variable is best measured and described. We compared these scales by fuel variable and then by sample site to evaluate if fuel properties are constant across study sites. We also evaluated whether the spatial variation in fuel variables is isotropic (same in all directions) or anisotropic (directional) (Maglione and Diblasi 2004), and we addressed whether the variation is stationary (homogeneous in space). Two spatial statistics were computed to describe the spatial structure of fuel variables: Moran's I and Geary's C. Spatial analysis was performed using the geoR spatial package (Ribeiro and Diggle 2001) in R statistical computing software. Because of the skewed distribution of the canopy fuel variables, a log transformation was performed, after adding a small constant. The best fitting theoretical model was performed through the use of authorized models (spherical, exponential, linear, and pure nugget), and the weighted least squares method was used as a fitting procedure in cases in which two or more theoretical variograms were found. The weight applied to each of the semi-variance estimates was proportional to the number of couples of data involved in that estimate (Cressie 1985; McBratney and Webster 1986). We used spatial dependence and variation analysis to determine the relationship of the ecosystem variables in Table 6 to the fuel variables.

Results

Results from this study are stratified by the sampled variability across the entire grid (Fuel Variability) and then by the spatial variability analyzed within the grid (Spatial Variability). Surface and canopy fuels are then summarized within these two broad variability categories. Because this study generated abundant data that created many diverse results, we mostly present general summary tables for the majority of the complex analysis in this study. To describe the important intermediate findings used to create these summary tables, we use detailed results from the Tenderfoot Forest (TF) study site to illustrate the how the statistics in the summary tables were derived.

Fuel Variability

Surface Fuels

Loading. Surface fuel characteristics were highly variable both within and across study sites (Table 7; Figure 10). For loading, it appears that the sampled variability was high across nearly all of the down woody fuel components with the larger fuel having the highest variabilities. One hour fuel loadings were low ranging from 0.005 (BV; see Table 1 for site acronyms) to 0.066 kg m^{-2} (TF) with high standard errors (0.005 at BV to 0.057 at TF) and high coefficients of variation (80 percent at CF to 187 percent at NM) (see Table 2 for sample site descriptions and codes). Loadings for 10 hr woody fuels were highest (0.009 kg m^{-2} for BV to 0.458 kg m^{-2} for LF) across all four downed woody fuel components for four sites (LF, TF, BV, and SM), probably as a result of management activities; as a consequence, the variability was also the highest with standard deviations ranging from 0.022 (BV) to 1.169 (LF) corresponding to ranges of 0.214 (BV) to 9.859 kg m^{-2} (LF), and IQR (25 to 75 percentile) from 0.01 (BV) to 0.264 (LF) kg m^{-2}. Interestingly, the highest coefficient of variations for 10 hr fuels did not occur on the sites with the highest fuel loadings and variance (range was from 132 percent for TF to 329 percent for SM). The larger 100 hr fuel loadings were similar in loading and variability across all sites except the sagebrush grassland BV site; excluding BV, 100 hr loadings ranged from 0.025 kg m^{-2} (SM) to 0.219 (NM) kg m^{-2}, deviations ranged from 0.11 (TF, SM) to 0.50 (NM) kg m^{-2}, IQR ranged from zero to 0.261 (NM) kg m^{-2}, and the similar coefficient of variation was around 250 percent (185 to 444 percent). The sagebrush grassland BV loadings were low and variable because sagebrush shrubs rarely produce woody material greater than 2.5 cm in diameter. Logs (1000 hr fuels) were rare across all sites but had some of the highest fuel loads (zero at BV to 0.57 kg m^{-2} in lodgepole pine forests at the TF), high deviations (zero to 0.707 kg m^{-2}), and the highest ranges (zero to 7.4 kg m^{-2} at SM), yet the coefficients of variations were approximately the same as the other woody fuel components (101 percent at NM to 603 percent at SM).

One important result is that the Levene test for equal variances showed strong evidence of differences between the population variance at each site for all fuel components except the herb, indicating that the variation of these surface fuels is quite different across sites and across components. Moreover, this variance across all downed woody classes is not normally distributed with skewness statistics well over 1.0 for most sites and components. Skewness statistics ranged from 2.0 for 1 hr loadings in the lodgepole (TF) forest to over 7.0 for 1000 hr fuels in the pine-fir-larch (LF) forest and 10 hr fuels in pine savanna (CF). Skewness was over 9.7 for logs on the pinyon-juniper (SM) site, indicating that there were many plots with small loading estimates and few plots with high loading estimates.

The live and dead shrub and herbaceous loads were perhaps the least variable of all surface fuels (Table 7; Figure 10). Shrub loadings ranged from 0.05 kg m^{-2} (sites LF, TF, CF) to 0.225 kg m^{-2} (sagebrush BV) with low deviations (0.042 kg m^{-2} in lodgepole TF to 0.187 kg m^{-2} in SM pinyon-juniper) and low ranges (0.194 kg m^{-2} in TF to 1.28 kg m^{-2} in SM; IQR ranged from 0.038 kg m^{-2} to 0.164 kg m^{-2}), and the variance was a small proportion of the mean (0.5 in BV to 2.0 at

Table 7. General statistics describing the variability of the surface fuel components across the six study sites. Number in parentheses under fuel component is the number of observations.

Fuel Attribute	Fuel Component	Mean	Standard Deviation	Range	Coefficient of Variation (CV)	Skewness	IQR
Lubrecht Forest (LF)							
Loading (kg m^{-2})	1 hour woody (125)	0.027	0.037	0.273	134.922	3.626	0.030
	10 hour woody (125)	0.458	1.169	9.859	255.345	5.728	0.264
	100 hour woody (125)	0.103	0.292	2.500	284.212	5.621	0.085
	1000 hour woody (125)	0.276	0.597	6.00	216.131	7.355	0.260
	Shrub (125)	0.056	0.064	0.409	113.626	3.115	0.045
	Herb (125)	0.032	0.019	0.146	59.039	3.486	0.014
	Litter+Duff (125)	11.379	6.654	35.616	58.473	1.393	7.518
	Entire fuelbed (125)	12.058	7.343	43.989	60.895	1.639	8.030
Particle density (kg m^{-3})	1 hour woody (22)	629.228	174.487	798.755	27.730	-0.566	181.180
	10 hour woody (28)	509.909	209.232	865.870	41.033	1.638	189.066
	100 hour woody (13)	326.899	226.709	702.471	69.351	0.322	433.896
	1000 hour woody (35)	195.884	60.443	261.975	30.857	0.178	85.650
Bulk density (kg m^{-3})	Shrub (185)	0.388	0.439	2.646	113.194	2.775	0.368
	Herb (218)	0.257	0.172	1.242	67.142	2.213	0.152
	Litter+Duff (24)	416.400	321.028	1088.208	77.096	0.982	437.342
Mineral content (%)	1 hour woody (25)	3.613	5.794	30.314	160.369	4.421	1.430
	10 hour woody (29)	1.048	0.678	2.859	64.696	1.683	0.692
	100 hour woody (9)	0.730	0.240	0.755	32.921	1.143	0.320
	1000 hour woody (10)	0.778	0.507	1.333	65.163	1.422	0.649
	Litter+Duff (34)	47.470	21.348	71.626	44.971	-0.442	38.953
Tenderfoot Forest (TF)							
Loading (kg m^{-2})	1 hour woody (124)	0.066	0.057	0.328	85.857	2.021	0.042
	10 hour woody (124)	0.136	0.179	1.293	131.747	3.792	0.141
	100 hour woody (124)	0.046	0.115	0.600	252.185	3.514	0.040
	1000 hour woody (123)	0.568	0.707	3.800	124.490	2.356	0.600
	Shrub (124)	0.053	0.042	0.194	78.628	1.312	0.051
	Herb (124)	0.027	0.020	0.150	73.383	2.482	0.030
	Litter+Duff (124)	4.704	3.046	18.551	64.743	1.795	3.417
	Entire fuelbed (124)	5.037	3.106	19.001	61.664	1.755	3.297
Particle density (kg m^{-3})	1 hour woody (27)	567.025	162.651	949.998	28.685	0.880	72.521
	10 hour woody (25)	498.520	90.985	366.413	18.251	0.117	103.074
	100 hour woody (7)	453.666	132.549	396.242	29.217	0.281	222.792
	1000 hour woody (38)	190.299	25.869	110.337	13.594	-0.241	39.659
Bulk density (kg m^{-3})	Shrub (212)	0.382	0.290	1.505	75.794	1.216	0.364
	Herb (213)	0.241	0.148	0.783	61.646	0.977	0.213
	Litter+Duff (30)	191.102	169.148	846.763	88.512	2.863	142.766
Mineral content (%)	1 hour woody (27)	1.583	1.189	5.341	75.117	2.527	0.792
	10 hour woody (23)	3.591	13.222	63.865	368.152	4.788	0.541
	100 hour woody (4)	0.758	0.316	0.674	41.611	0.054	0.600
	1000 hour woody (7)	0.510	0.165	0.463	32.419	1.548	0.181
	Litter+Duff (30)	28.441	19.161	63.324	67.370	0.902	27.328
Ninemile (NM)							
Loading (kg m^{-2})	1 hour woody (120)	0.023	0.044	0.389	187.886	5.609	0.017
	10 hour woody (120)	0.198	0.410	3.155	207.272	4.699	0.113
	100 hour woody (120)	0.219	0.501	4.578	228.263	6.173	0.261
	1000 hour woody (120)	0.377	0.386	2.600	101.328	2.183	0.500
	Shrub (120)	0.076	0.081	0.454	105.949	2.904	0.058
	Herb (120)	0.041	0.020	0.104	48.796	0.812	0.020
	Litter+Duff (120)	4.459	2.988	18.815	67.006	2.128	2.757
	Entire fuelbed (120)	5.016	3.430	20.415	68.374	2.278	2.867

Table 7. *Continued.*

Fuel Attribute	Fuel Component	Mean	Standard Deviation	Range	Coefficient of Variation (CV)	Skewness	IQR
		Ninemile (NM)					
Particle density (kg m⁻³)	21)	606 59	125 187	548 027	20 65	-0 897	104 759
	2)	553 432	20 092	1027 321	36 15	3 01	98 37
	4)	519 86	88 084	275 05	16 944	-0 405	153 4 3
	(19)	178 130	55 634	203 496	3 232	0 33	89 744
Bulk density (kg m⁻³)	203	0 633	1 99	14 748	7 61	10 7	.450
	21	0 629	5 628	82 713	894 363	14 65	153
	Litter+Duff (25)	148 696	120.347	598.811	80.935	2.838	98.197
Mineral ontent (%)	1 ho r woody (21)	2 043	0 668	2 303	32 701	-0 363	1 58
	10 hour woody (23)	1 540	0.550	1.810	35.694	-0.396	1.015
	0 hour w dy (6	0 552	0 198	0 515	35 804	- 486	0 31
	1000 hour woody (5)	0 672	0.242	0.534	36.001	-0.001	0.476
	Duff (25)	14 640	9 136	29 136	62 402	453	1 187
	L tte (25)	33 499	16.087	51.247	48.022	0.220	29.622
		Bighole Valley (BV)					
L adi g kg m⁻²)	1 hour woody (124)	0.005	0 05	0 027	100 61	2 555	0.003
	0 hour w dy (124)	0 009	0 022	2	24 723	6 5 9	0 01
	0 hour w dy (124)	0 004	029	0 300	776 240	9 396	.000
	0 hour w dy	*No logs were found on any plots*					
	Shrub (124)	0.225	110	0 686	49 054	280	087
	Herb (124)	0.044	0 112	0 978	251 382	6 867	0 024
	Litter+Duff (124)	0 210	0 221	1.045	105.549	1.851	0.201
	Entire fuelbed (124)	0.497	0.323	1.801	64.982	1.633	0.262
Particle density (kg m⁻³)	1 hour woody (21)	595.585	111.023	515.873	18.641	2.709	64.699
	10 hour woody (2)	597.330	107.264	151.694	17.957	*Not enough data*	
	100 hour wood	*No fuel particles were found on subsampled microplots*					
	1000 hour woody	*No logs were found on any plots*					
Bulk density (kg m⁻³)	Shrub (216)	1 833	1 79	19 4 4	97 630	5 1 6	1.26
	Herb (223)	0 331	0 723	7 7 2	218 699	8 484	0 2 1
	it er+Duff (30)	153 426	214 647	1097 277	139 903	3 209	200 613
Mineral content (%)	9	8 311	3 303	13 172	39 742	741	4 356
	10 hour woody (22)	7.999	2.817	12.747	35.214	1.004	3.552
		No fuel particles were found on subsampled microplots					
	1000 hour woody	*No logs were found on any plots*					
	L tte +Duff (30)	46 931	17 401	54 870	37 079	-0 469	29 916
		Silver Mountain (SM)					
L adi g (kg m⁻²)	1 hour woody (123)	00 8	0 009	0 061	109 691	3.0 7	0 00
	0 hour w dy (123)	0 025	00 2	0 654	328 7 9	6. 9	026
	0 hour w dy (123)	0 025	0 110	1 000	444 586	6.729	000
	0 hour w dy (123)	113	685	7 400	603 67	9.751	018
	Shrub (123)	092	87	1 283	20 76	3.7 5	64
	Herb (123)	0 01	0 089	1 000	846 729	11.155	0 001
	Litter+Duff (123)	1.431	2.141	16.603	149.595	3.470	2.037
	Entire fuelbed (123)	1 556	2 190	16 668	40 741	3.230	2 201
Particle density (kg m⁻³)	1 hour woody (26)	657.414	119.498	466 667	18.177	0.689	182.13
	10 hour woody (5)	632.553	31.303	74.297	4.949	-2.144	40.891
	100 hour woody (0)	*No fuel particles were found on subsampled microplots*					
	1000 hour woody (30)	521.628	75.295	360.330	14.435	-0.147	94.512
Bulk density (kg m⁻³)	Shrub (48)	1.105	0.894	5 053	80.833	2.566	0.928
	Herb (122)	1 782	1 734	99 996	714 62	7.708	0 073
	it er+Duff (22)	339 8	976 524	4784 88	287 68	4.693	188 08
Mineral content (%)	1 hour woody (29)	3.262	2.732	16.553	83.759	-0.509	2.259
	10 hour woody (10)	4.249	2.918	9.433	68.671	1.837	3.196
	100 hour woody (0)	*No fuel particles were found on subsampled microplots*					
	1000 hour woody (10)	1.097	0.371	1.038	33.832	0.709	0.618
	Litter+Duff (27)	41.190	23.509	93.519	57.075	0.375	41.697

Table 7. *Continued.*

Fuel Attribute	Fuel Component	Mean	Standard Deviation	Range	Coefficient of Variation (CV)	Skewness	IQR
Colville Forest (CF)							
Loading (kg m⁻²)	1 hour woody (111)	0.017	0.014	0.076	80.049	2.250	0.010
	10 hour woody (111)	0.078	0.150	1.440	193.649	7.039	0.037
	100 hour woody (111)	0.082	0.152	0.800	185.399	2.480	0.100
	1000 hour woody (111)	0.657	0.685	4.200	105.532	2.117	0.777
	Shrub (111)	0.055	0.097	0.951	176.966	7.073	0.038
	Herb (111)	0.056	0.025	0.164	44.417	0.948	0.035
	Litter+Duff (111)	2.546	1.322	7.124	51.930	0.239	1.614
	Entire fuelbed (111)	2.745	1.491	7.540	54.310	0.243	1.691
Particle density (kg m⁻³)	1 hour woody (19)	493.475	45.402	132.103	9.201	-0.101	87.505
	10 hour woody (11)	482.016	76.071	281.294	15.782	0.151	98.342
	100 hour woody	No Data					
	1000 hour woody (40)	348.273	102.038	399.177	29.298	0.220	162.637
Bulk density (kg m⁻³)	Shrub (159)	0.671	0.545	3.460	81.155	1.574	0.730
	Herb (207)	0.210	0.157	1.068	74.575	2.328	0.161
	Litter+Duff (30)	66.132	41.798	168.133	63.203	0.789	61.326
Mineral content (%)	1 hour woody (24)	1.239	0.968	5.263	78.112	3.288	0.652
	10 hour woody (23)	0.889	0.382	1.401	42.933	0.641	0.626
	100 hour woody (6)	0.604	0.126	0.365	20.846	-0.661	0.202
	1000 hour woody (10)	0.609	0.189	0.576	31.055	-0.103	0.362
	Litter+Duff (30)	22.152	12.485	51.851	56.361	0.924	21.064

SM). The sagebrush-grassland site (BV) had the highest shrub and herb loadings and variance, but for shrubs, variance was only half the mean, yet the variance of the herb loading was 2.5 times the mean. Herb loadings were low for all sites (0.011 kg m⁻² at SM to 0.056 kg m⁻² at CF) with correspondingly low standard deviations and ranges (0.019 to 0.112 kg m⁻² and IQR of 0.001 to 0.035 kg m⁻²). Coefficient of variation values were below 100 percent for all but two sites; the sagebrush grassland (BV) was 251 percent and the pinyon juniper (SM) woodland was 850 percent. Similar to down woody fuels, loadings of shrub and herbs were positively skewed toward plots with high fuel loadings (skewness statistic ranged from 0.8 to 11.0 for herbs and 1.3 to 7.0 for shrubs). Herb loadings were the most skewed, while shrubs tended to have skewness statistics around 3.0 for many sites.

The highest loads were typically found in the litter+duff fuel component ranging from 0.2 kg m⁻² (BV) to 11 3 kg m⁻² (LF), and these loads usually comprised over 90 percent of the total fuelbed load. These loads had a high standard error (0.22 to 6.6 kg m⁻²), but they also had a low coefficient of variation (58 to 149 percent) with respect to the other fuel components. The high loads at LF were due to the high bulk density values (average of 416 kg m⁻³) measured for this site, which was probably a result of the harvest residues containing many woody particles embedded in the litter+duff profile. Duff and litter loading was the least skewed with statistics ranging from 0.2 to 3 5, indicating that this is the only fuel component where loadings may be normally distributed.

Overall, it appears that fuel component loadings were rarely correlated with each other (Table 8). While most correlation coefficients were significant ($p < 0.05$), the highest correlation was 0 41 between 10 and 100 hr fine woody fuels. All others were well below 0.3 and were both positive and negative, indicating a general lack of correlation across surface fuel components. Interestingly, log loadings were especially unrelated to all other fuel loadings with coefficients ranging from -0.07 for logs to shrub correlations to 0.23 for logs to 10 hr woody fuel.

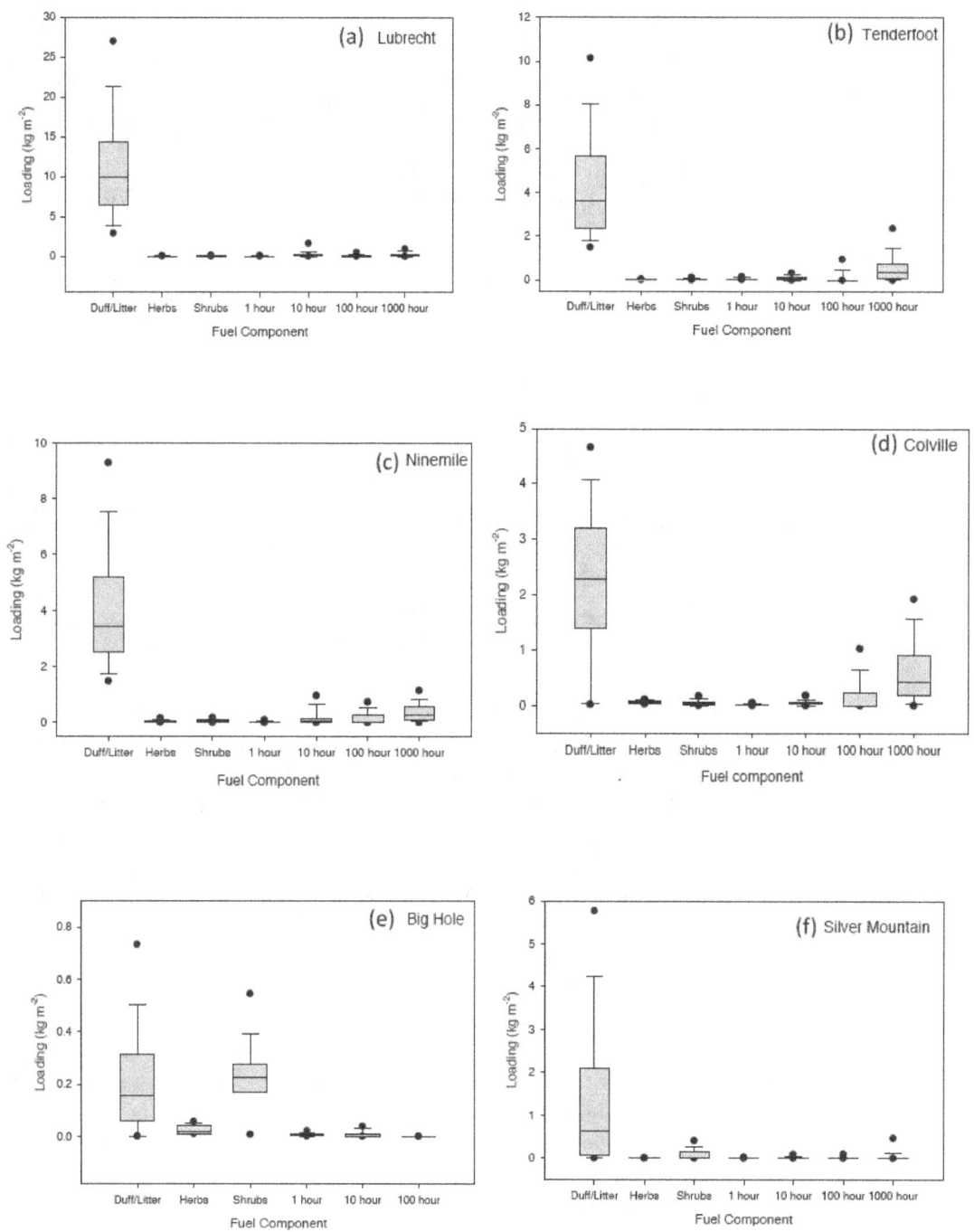

Figure 10. Box and whisker plots of the loadings (kg m^{-2}) of each surface fuel component across all sampled sites: (a) Lubrecht Forest, (b) Tenderfoot Forest, (c) Ninemile, (d) Colville Forest, (e) Bighole Valley, and (f) Silver Mountain.

Table 8. Pearson's correlation table for surface fuel loadings for all plots across all sites.

Surface Fuel Component	Surface Fuel Component					
	1 hour	10 hour	100 hour	Shrubs	Herbs	Litter+Duff
10 hour	0.197*** (n = 1321)					
100 hour	0.150*** (n = 1322)	0.408*** (n = 1321)				
Shrubs	-0.088*** (n = 1321)	-0.074*** (n = 1323)	-0.048* (n = 1322)			
Herbs	-0.001 (n = 1322)	-0.009 (n = 1320)	0.075*** (n = 1321)	0.246*** (n = 1321)		
Litter+Duff	0.174*** (n = 1322)	0.334*** (n = 1321)	0.265*** (n = 1322)	-0.193*** (n = 1322)	0.007 (n = 1321)	
Logs	0.074* (n = 599)	0.231*** (n = 600)	0.088** (n = 599)	-0.066 (n = 600)	0.128*** (n = 599)	0.081** (n = 600)

*significant at .10

**significant at .05

***significant at .01

Particle Density. While not as variable as loadings, the density of wood particles was different by fuel component and sample site (Table 7). In general, wood particle densities usually decreased as particle diameter increased, and, as expected, wood particle density was more variable across sites than fuel components. Densities of 1 hr particles ranged from 493 kg m^{-3} (CF) to 657 kg m^{-3} (SM) with standard deviations that were from 9 percent to 28 percent of the mean (45 kg m^{-3} at CF to 163 kg m^{-3} at TF). The ranges and IQR were also small (65 to 182 kg m^{-3}), and particle densities for this fuel component were also the most highly skewed (skewness ranging from -0.1 to 2.7). Particle densities were quite high for these fine woody fuels and probably reflect the difficulty of measuring volume on these small twigs.

The 10 and 100 hr fuels showed the highest variation across sites with means that were the closest to documented densities of sound wood. Particle densities of 10 hr fuels ranged from 482 kg m^{-3} at the CF pine savanna to over 632 kg m^{-3} at the pinyon-juniper SM site (Table 7) with corresponding deviations of 31 kg m^{-3} (SM) to 209 kg m^{-3} (LF), ranges of 74 kg m^{-3} (SM) to over 1000 kg m^{-3} (NM), and IQRs of 41 (SM) to over 189 (LF). However, this variation was not a significant portion of the mean with coefficients of variation ranging from 5 (SM) to 41 percent (LF). Only three sites had 100 hr fuel particles, but these sites had the highest variabilities with means ranging from 326 kg m^{-3} (LF) to 519 kg m^{-3} (NM), standard deviations from 88 to 226 kg m^{-3}, and ranges from 275 to 702 kg m^{-3}. And like other fuel components, this variability in 100 hr fuels was not a significant portion of the mean (16 percent at NM to 69 at LF). The 100 hr fuel particle densities were the one fuel characteristic that was mostly normally distributed with skewness statistics between -1.0 and 1.0.

Logs had the lowest particle densities (178 kg m^{-3} at NM to 523 kg m^{-3} for SM) with the lowest deviations (25 kg m^{-3} for TF to 102 kg m^{-3} for CF) that were around 4 to 30 percent of the mean. Log densities also seemed to be somewhat normally distributed (skewness between -0.2 to 0.2) in a narrow range of sampled values. Most sites had log densities below 200 kg m^{-3} (LF, TF, NM), reflecting the high proportion of rotten logs in the sample.

Bulk Density. Shrub layer bulk densities were surprisingly low in variability across sites when compared with woody fuel particle densities (Table 7). Shrub layer bulk densities ranged from 0.67 kg m^{-3} at the CF pine grassland savanna to over 1.8 kg m^{-3} for the sagebrush grassland BV site. Variability statistics were somewhat low with low deviations (0.29 kg m^{-3} for grouse whortleberry at TF to 1.7 kg m^{-3} at the sagebrush BV site), high ranges (1.5 kg m^{-3} at TF to over 14 kg m^{-3} at NM), and low IQR (0.36 kg m^{-3} at LF to 1.3 kg m^{-3} at BV), indicating a few plots containing high abundance of shrubs at each site. This variability was around 90 percent of the mean (coefficient of variation ranged from 75 percent for TF to 113 percent for LF) and highly skewed from normal (skewness from 1.2 to 10.7).

Herb layer bulk densities were similar in magnitude to shrubs ranging from 0.21 kg m^{-3} in the pine savanna of CF to 1.78 kg m^{-3} in the SM pinyon-juniper, and they were also as variable across sites (Table 7). Standard deviations and ranges were lowest (0.15 kg m^{-3} and 0.78 kg m^{-3}, respectively) on the grouse whortleberry understory of TF and the pine-grass savanna of CF and highest on the SM pinyon-juniper site (12.7 kg m^{-3} and 99.99 kg m^{-3}, respectively). This variation was around 70 percent of the mean for three sites (LF, TF, and CF), but was over 200 percent for the other three (BV was at 219 percent, NM was at 894 percent, and SM was over 700 percent). Herb bulk densities were more skewed than shrubs with ranges from 0.98 to 14.65 and 1.20 to 10.75, respectively.

The litter+duff bulk densities were much higher than shrub and herb layer bulk densities, but their variabilities were quite similar. Duff and litter bulk densities were high, ranging from 66 kg m^{-3} in the pine needle-grass layer of CF to 416 kg m^{-3} in the logging residue pine-fir-larch stand of LF. The litter+duff layer bulk density deviations were quite variable from 42 kg m^{-3} in the homogeneous pine-grass of CF to 976 kg m^{-3} at the highly discontinuous pinyon-juniper SM site, and the span of bulk densities were only 168 at CF to over 1000 kg m^{-3} at three sites with discontinuous litter+duff layers (LF, BV, and SM where the range was over 4000 kg m^{-3}). While this range is somewhat large, the deviation was mostly less than 100 percent of the mean (coefficient of variations ranged from 63 in the pine savanna of CF to over 287 at the SM pinyon-juniper). Skewness statistics were well above 0.5, indicating a high number of dense litter+duff layer measurements.

Mineral Content. Of all the fuel characteristics, the percent mineral content was the least variable within a site but it did tend to vary across fuel components and across sites (Table 7). One hour fuel particles had the highest mineral contents for the downed woody fuels, ranging from 1.2 percent at CF to 8.3 percent at BV, while the 10 hr woody fuels were the most variable (over 300 percent coefficient of variation on TF). Logs had the lowest mineral contents (less than 1 percent), but their coefficients of variation were comparable to the fine woody fuels (31 percent to 65 percent at LF). The BV sagebrush grassland easily had the highest mineral contents of all woody fuel components (greater than 8 percent), while the CF pine savanna had the lowest contents (less than 1.2 percent). The three Montana forest sites (LF, TF, NM) had comparable mineral contents across all woody fuel components (approximately 1 to 4 percent for 1 hr, 1 to 3 percent for 100 hr, 0.5 to 0.8 percent for 100 hr, and 0.6 to 0.7 for 1000 hr). Overall, woody fuel mineral contents were moderately variable, having coefficient of variations that hovered around 50 percent of the mean with small ranges (IQR values from 0.1 to 1.0 percent).

Litter+duff mineral contents were often an order of magnitude higher than woody fuel mineral contents, ranging from 22 percent for the CF pine savanna

Table 9. Description of canopy fuel variability for canopy loading, canopy bulk density, and canopy cover for general variability descriptions for all sites with a tree layer (Bighole Valley site was sagebrush grassland with no canopy fuels).

Measure of Variability	Canopy Loading	Canopy Bulk Density	Canopy Cover
Units	$(kg\ m^{-3})$	$(kg\ m^{-2})$	(percent)
Silver Mountain (SM) Pinyon Juniper			
Mean	0.83	0.28	29.84
Range	2.17	0.74	57.38
Standard Deviation	0.51	0.18	15.04
Coefficient of Variation	0.61	0.65	0.50
Skewness	0.62	0.71	0.23
IQR	0.77	0.27	22.90
Number Observations (n)	124	124	124
Colville Forest (CF) Ponderosa Pine Savanna			
Mean	0.15	0.02	15.75
Range	0.45	0.06	24.41
Standard Deviation	0.08	0.01	5.34
Coefficient of Variation	0.52	0.53	0.34
Skewness	1.06	2.15	0.69
IQR	0.12	0.01	5.09
Number Observations (n)	69	69	69
Ninemile (NM) Ponderosa Pine-Douglas-Fir			
Mean	0.70	0.08	35.82
Range	1.77	0.21	51.64
Standard Deviation	0.34	0.05	11.70
Coefficient of Variation	0.49	0.57	0.33
Skewness	1.00	1.02	0.11
IQR	0.46	0.06	18.24
Number Observations (n)	120	120	120
Lubrecht Forest (LF) Ponderosa Pine-Douglas-Fir-Larch			
Mean	0.58	0.06	34.20
Range	1.75	0.19	55.17
Standard Deviation	0.29	0.04	11.30
Coefficient of Variation	0.49	0.59	0.33
Skewness	1.33	1.65	0.27
IQR	0.34	0.04	13.62
Number Observations (n)	123	123	123
Tenderfoot Forest (TF) Lodgepole Pine			
Mean	0.83	0.13	43.85
Range	1.11	0.34	49.98
Standard Deviation	0.21	0.06	8.89
Coefficient of Variation	0.26	0.48	0.20
Skewness	-0.15	1.03	-0.35
IQR	0.28	0.08	11.56
Number Observations (n)	123	123	123

a. Canopy fuel load CFL

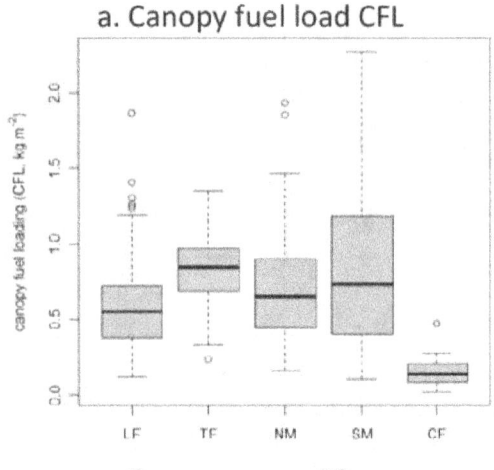

b. Canopy bulk density CBD

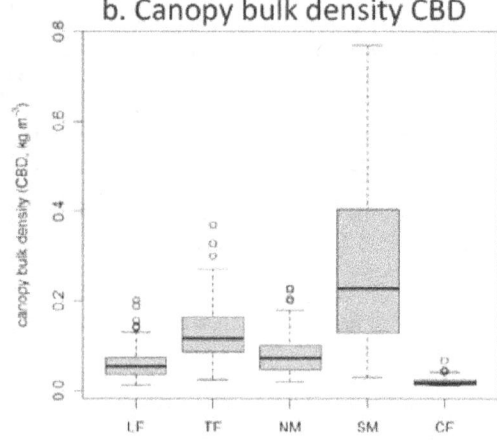

c. Canopy cover CC

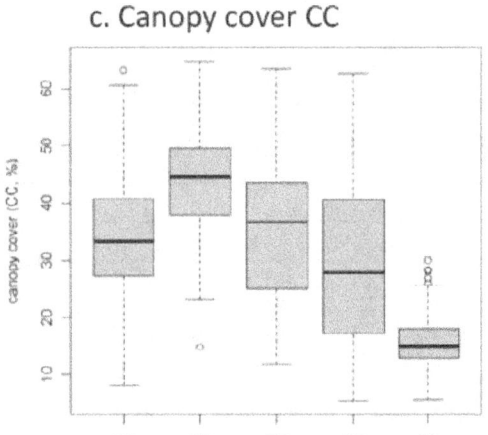

Figure 11. Box and whisker plots of the three canopy fuel characteristics (a) canopy fuel loading (CFL, kg m^{-2}); (b) canopy bulk density (CBD, kg m^{-3}); and (c) canopy cover (CC, %) across all sites: Lubrecht Forest (LF), Tenderfoot Forest (TF), Ninemile (NM), Silver Mountain (SM), and Colville Forest (CF). Bighole Valley (BV) site was sagebrush grassland with no canopy fuels.

to over 47 percent in the LF pine-fir-larch thinning unit (Table 7). These duff and litter layers also had the greatest variation in range (51 to 93 percent), IQR (21 percent at CF to 42 percent at SM), and coefficient of variation (37 percent at BV to 67 percent at TF). Sites that had thinning and grazing activity seemed to have the highest mineral contents (SM, BV, LF).

Canopy Fuels

Canopy fuel characteristics were quite similar across sites and across all three variables (Table 9; Figure 11). Perhaps the most important canopy characteristic to fire management, CBD, ranged from 0.02 to 0.28 kg m^{-3} with standard deviations from 0.01 to 0.18, but coefficients of variation ranged from only 48 to 65 percent. The range of the data, as measured by IQR, was also quite similar (0.01 to 0.08 kg m^{-3}), except for the SM site, which had a high IQR of 0.271 because of the discontinuous canopy of the pinyon-juniper forest type. The BV sagebrush-grassland site had no canopy fuels on any of the plots within that grid.

It appears canopy fuels are highly correlated to some stand characteristics (Table 10), but they have little relationship with surface fuels (Table 11). Most canopy fuel characteristics were correlated to basal area and tree density and less correlated to average tree diameter and height with most of correlation coefficients

Table 10. Pearson's correlation results for the three canopy fuel characteristics across all plots in all sites for the stand level variables.

	Average DBH (cm)	Average Tree Height (m)	Overstory Basal Area (m^2 ha^{-1})	Trees Density (trees ha^{-1})
Lubrecht Forest (LF) Ponderosa Pine-Douglas-Fir-Larch				
Canopy loading (kg m^{-2})	-0.207*	-0.260**	0.663***	0.530***
Canopy bulk density (kg m^{-3})	-0.307**	-0.322**	0.595***	0.583***
Canopy cover (%)	-0.437***	-0.316**	0.854***	0.830***
Tenderfoot Forest (TF) Lodgepole Pine				
Canopy loading (kg m^{-2})	-0.229*	0.173	0.822***	0.853***
Canopy bulk density (kg m^{-3})	-0.210*	0.238**	0.714***	0.819***
Canopy cover (%)	-0.286**	0.121	0.842***	0.905***
Ninemile (NM) Ponderosa Pine-Douglas-Fir				
Canopy loading (kg m^{-2})	0.131	0.020	0.773***	0.709***
Canopy bulk density (kg m^{-3})	0.054	0.003	0.638***	0.620***
Canopy cover (%)	0.078	-0.041	0.906***	0.861***
Silver Mountain (SM) Pinyon Juniper				
Canopy loading (kg m^{-2})	0.590***	0.068	0.982***	0.894***
Canopy bulk density (kg m^{-3})	0.497***	-0.095	0.928***	0.921***
Canopy cover (%)	0.545***	0.037	0.946***	0.930***
Colville Forest (CF) Ponderosa Pine Savanna				
Canopy loading (kg m^{-2})	0.061	0.051	0.199	0.110
Canopy bulk density (kg m^{-3})	-0.165	-0.116	0.480***	0.664***
Canopy cover (%)	-0.045	0.100	0.805***	0.795***

*p value<0.1, **p value<0.05, ***p value<0.01

Table 11. Pearson's correlation table showing relationships between surface fuel loading and canopy fuel and stand characteristics using values for all plots across all sites (n = 167).

Fuel Component	Canopy Loading (kg m^{-2})	Canopy Bulk Density (kg m^{-3})	Canopy Cover (%)	Average DBH (cm)	Average Tree Height (m)	Overstory Basal Area (m^2 ha^{-1})	Trees per Hectare (m^2 ha^{-1})
Surface fuel components (n = 320)							
1 hour	0.109**	-0.069	0.259***	-0.16***	0.243***	0.383***	0.346***
10 hour	-0.034	-0.105**	0.044	0.003	0.116***	0.041	-0.021
100 hour	-0.001	-0.079*	0.039	0.123***	0.141***	0.042	-0.07*
1000 hour	-0.037	-0.111***	0.051	-0.158***	0.155***	0.098**	0.103**
Herbs	-0.021	-0.06	-0.007	0.103**	0.19***	0.042	-0.087**
Shrubs	-0.124***	-0.087**	-0.177***	0.019	-0.09**	-0.157***	-0.132**
Litter+Duff	-0.05	-0.245***	0.15***	0.102**	0.376***	0.203***	0.004
Canopy fuel characteristics (n = 559)							
CFL, Fuel loading	1.000	0.791***	0.875***	0.069	0.010	0.688***	0.619***
CBD, Bulk density	0.791***	1.000	0.521***	-0.026	-0.058	0.671***	0.721***
CC, Cover	0.875***	0.521***	1.000	-0.029	-0.020	0.871***	0.864***

*p value<0.1, **p value<0.05, ***p value<0.01

significant, but these correlations were quite different across sites (Tables 10, 11). The highest correlations were for canopy cover to basal area across all sites, which ranged from 0.84 to 0.95, while the lowest coefficients were for tree height to all three canopy variables, which ranged from -0.32 to 0.24 across all sites. The SM pinyon juniper site had the highest correlations overall, ranging from 0.50 to 0.95 excluding the tree height variable. Correlations of all canopy fuel and stand variables to the surface fuel loadings were low (<0.38), especially for coarse woody debris, shrubs, herbs, and litter+duff (Table 11). The highest correlations (>0.2) were relationships of 1 hr fuel loadings to canopy cover and all three stand characteristics. Canopy fuel characteristics were highly correlated with each other with coefficients ranging from 0.7 to 0.99 (Table 11).

Spatial Variability

Surface Fuel Loadings

Semivariograms of loading (kg m^{-2}) for the seven surface fuel components sampled at the TF study site are shown to illustrate the complexity of fitting semivariograms for each fuel component across different sites (Figure 12). Semivariance values are highly variable across each of the distances in the study (Figure 12), as shown by the scatter of the points used to build the model. Most sites had excellent fits (NM, LF, TF) while the CF pine savanna site had a poor fit with widely scattered semivariances. Exponential models were used for the three Montana sites, but the lack of distance-semivariance relationships for CF and SM required the use of a Gaussian or pure nugget model.

Statistics from the semivariograms arranged across the six sites showed some interesting relationships (Table 12). In general, all spatial statistics (range, sill, and nugget) seemed to increase with fuel particle diameter (Figure 13). The litter+duff, shrub, and herb are the components with the smallest particle diameters, and their spatial statistics are quite different across sites. Litter+duff had both the lowest (0.058) and the highest values for the sill, indicating a great disparity of spatial variance across sites for this component. Shrub fuels show similar behavior in that low values (less than 0.7 value) were present on all but the shrubby pinyon-juniper SM site where sill value exceeded 2.0. In contrast, herb fuels had some of the lowest spatial variance with sills ranging from 0.08 to 0.67 in semivariance. Downed woody fuels showed somewhat predictable behavior in that the semivariance was usually positively correlated with the size of the woody particle (1hr → 10 hr → 100 hr), except for 1000 hr fuels, for which the semivariance generally decreased. Sill values for 1 hr fuels (0.03 to 0.52) were generally lower than 10 hr fuels (0.35 to 2.18) which were generally lower than 100 hr fuels (0.74 to 3.59), but values for the 1000 hr fuels (0.05 to 2.13) were more similar to 10 hr fuels and did not increase over 100 hr fuels. This is in direct contrast to the general variability where 1000 hr fuels had the highest standard deviations, but those deviations were less than 50 percent of the mean (Table 7).

Nugget values were confusing and did not provide any additional information about spatial fuel variability because it was difficult to fit semivariograms with the data collected in this project. Nugget values usually indicate the amount of error involved in the measurement of the response variable, in this case fuel loading. However, many sites and components had nugget values at or near zero (Table 12). Loading measurements of fine woody debris (1, 10, 100 hr) were the most variable because they were quantified by corrected visual estimates, yet nugget values were the lowest for these components. The highest nugget values (1.1 and 1.7) were for

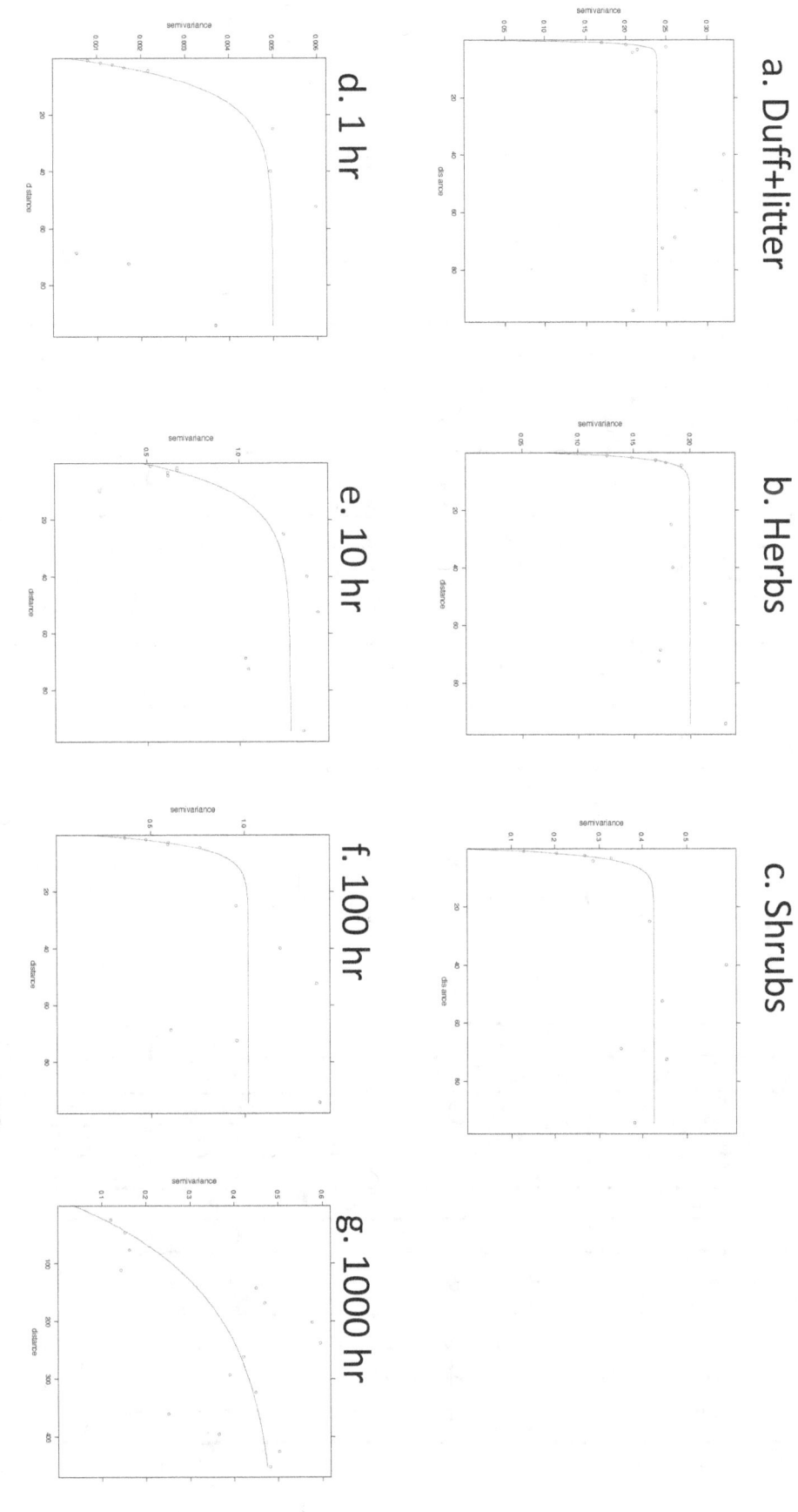

Figure 12. Semivariograms for the surface fuel characteristics measured on the Tenderfoot (TF) site: (a) duff+litter, (b) herbs, (c) shrubs, (d) 1 hr, (e) 10 hr, (f) 100 hr, and (g) 1000 hr.

Table 12. Semivariogram statistics for all surface fuel components across the six sites.

Fuel Component	Bighole Valley (BV) Sagebrush Grassland	Silver Mountain (SM) Pinyon Juniper	Colville Forest (CF) Pine Savannah	Ninemile (NM) Pine-Fir	Lubrecht Forest (LF) Pine-Fir-Larch	Tenderfoot Forest (TF) Lodgepole Pine
Sill (kg m^{-2})^2						
1 hour	0.128	0.174	0.282	0.051	0.029	0.524
10 hour	0.350	0.917	0.744	2.188	1.825	1.274
100 hour	No 100 hr	0.736	3.590	3.510	2.689	1.018
1000 hour	No Logs	2.129	1.967	0.055	1.825	1.778
Shrub	0.657	2.040	0.302	0.634	0.390	0.426
Herb	0.175	0.480	0.140	0.671	0.080	0.200
Litter+Duff	0.058	2.770	3.590	0.268	0.445	0.249
Nugget (kg m^{-2})^2						
1 hour	0.072	0.019	0.052	0.007	0.008	0.085
10 hour	0.121	0.000	0.000	1.500	0.575	0.478
100 hour	No 100 hr	0.053	2.260	1.430	0.449	0.190
1000 hour	No Logs	1.142	0.377	0.000	1.700	0.000
Shrub	0.389	0.000	0.000	0.000	0.050	0.000
Herb	0.000	0.000	0.000	0.103	0.000	0.073
Litter+Duff	0.059	0.000	2.260	0.115	0.000	0.016
Range (m)						
1 hour	4.67	2.50	2.83	16.30	8.90	6.02
10 hour	6.60	2.46	0.88	4.95	2.23	11.10
100 hour	No 100 hr	2.46	2.54	4.56	2.41	4.14
1000 hour	No Logs	No Logs	84.01	22.01	87.30	157.01
Shrub	2.44	15.10	0.85	1.79	3.61	2.66
Herb	0.72	1.11	0.80	3.50	0.52	1.83
Litter+Duff	0.45	1.41	2.54	1.29	0.48	0.85
Moran's I (p value)						
1 hour	*0.217	*0.157	0.060	*0.184	*0.242	*0.333
10 hour	*0.087	*0.109	0.021	-0.010	0.066	0.068
100 hour	No 100 hr	0.048	0.084	0.050	0.030	0.069
1000 hour	No Logs	-0.004	*0.045	*0.041	-0.007	*0.024
Shrub	0.022	*0.400	*0.074	0.018	*0.262	*0.138
Herb	0.023	0.014	*0.160	-0.012	*0.122	*0.130
Litter+Duff	0.064	*0.130	0.117	*0.124	*0.146	*0.219
Geary's C (p value)						
1 hour	*0.90	*0.94	*0.95	*0.76	*0.79	*0.942
10 hour	*0.93	*0.86	0.96	0.97	*0.88	*0.91
100 hour	No 100 hr	0.99	1.03	*0.91	0.97	*0.93
1000 hour	No Logs	*0.88	*0.87	*0.82	1.01	0.93
Shrub	0.99	*0.73	*0.81	*0.89	*0.53	*0.93
Herb	*0.95	0.99	0.95	0.96	1.01	*0.94
Litter+Duff	0.96	*0.92	0.98	*0.84	0.99	*0.81

*p value<0.1

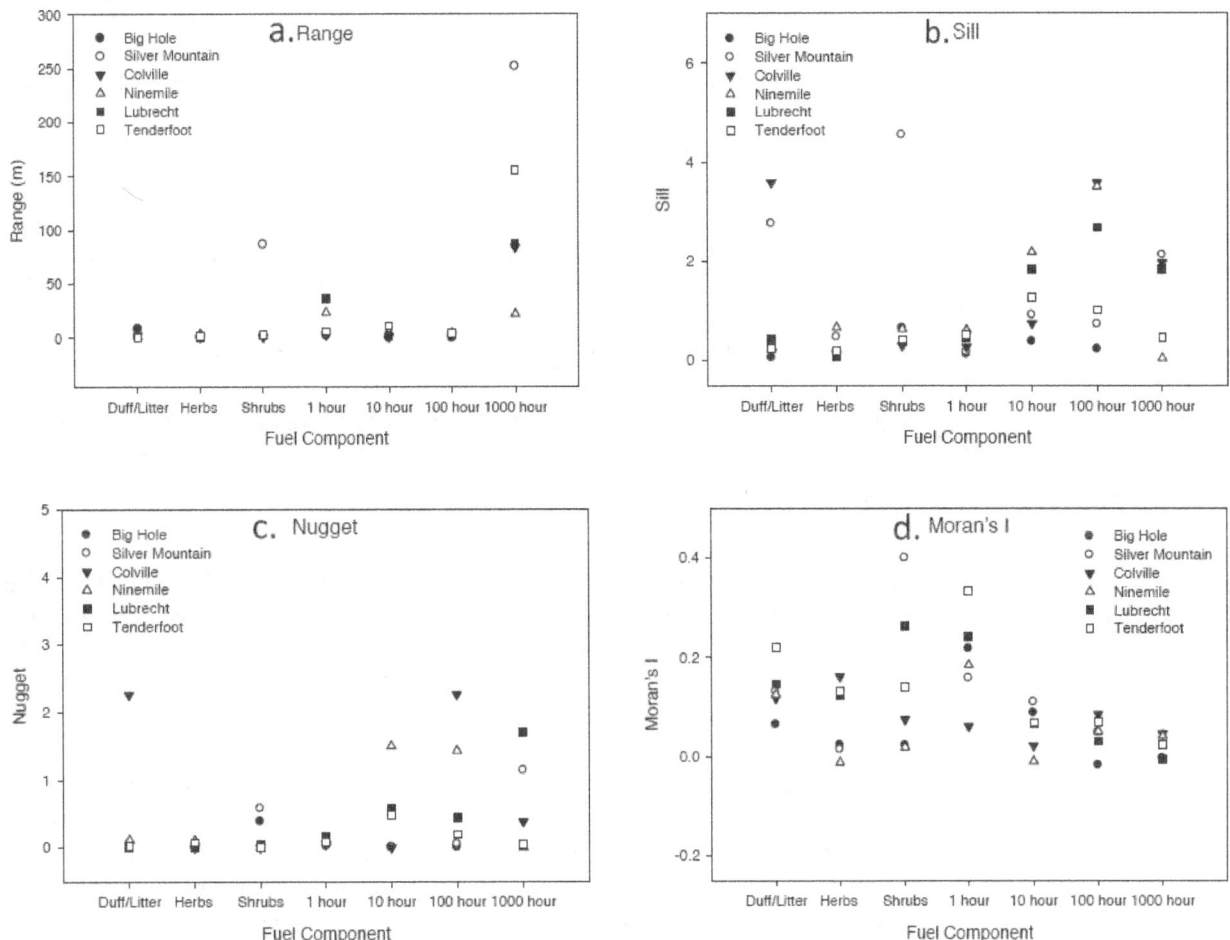

Figure 13. Spatial semivariogram statistics for each fuel component across all sites.

logs, which were the easiest to measure but were rarer in occurrence within the sampling grid. Litter+duff had both the highest (2.26) and the lowest (0.0) nugget values.

The range statistics provided the most important information on the spatial dynamics of surface and canopy fuels because range values indicate the inherent patch size of the measured entity (Table 12; Figure 13). Overall, it appears that the range generally increased with fuel size. Litter+duff ranges were the lowest and scaled from 0.5 m at LF pine-fir-larch to 2.5 m at CF pine savanna. Herbs had the next lowest patch size with ranges from 0.5 m (LF) to 3.5 m (NM), both pine-fir sites. Shrub fuels appeared to vary at the next highest scale with ranges from 0.9 m (CF) to 3.5 m (LF) and a large range of 15 m at SM indicating higher discontinuity in shrub-dominated pinyon-juniper. Fine woody fuels varied at about the same or greater patch sizes with 1 hr fuel ranges from 2.5 m (SM) to 16.3 m at LF, 10 hr ranges from 0.9 at CF to 11 m at TF, and 100 hr ranges from 2.4 m to 4.5 m (patch sizes are more variable with smaller particle diameters). Logs (1000 hr) fuels had the highest patch sizes ranging from 22 m at NM to 157 m at SM. We performed extensive statistical analysis relating the semivariogram range of each surface fuel component to the four measures of variance (standard deviation, range, IQR, and coefficient of variation) and found no significant relationships (Figure 16).

Most sites and fuel components had low Moran's I values (<0.2) and Geary C values near 1.0, indicating that there was little spatial structure in the northern Rocky Mountain fuelbeds sampled in this study (Table 12). The highest Moran's I values tended to be found in fine fuels, especially shrubs (0.3 at LF and 0.4 at SM) and 1 hr woody (0.24 for LF and 0.33 for TF), for which these values were statistically significant (p<0.05). Logs had the least spatial structure, with the Moran's I statistic less than 0.05 on all sites. Litter+duff results unexpectedly showed Moran's I less than 0.2 for all sites because this layer is somewhat homogeneous and often exhibits some spatial structure over small distances. Geary's C values showed nearly the same results even though this statistic was supposed to adjust for local settings (Table 12). The components with the least spatial structure were large woody fuel components (10, 100, 1000 hr components) and litter+duff because they had Geary's C values between 0.95 and 1.05, but fine fuels, such as 1 hr, shrub, and herbs, tended to have more spatial structure (values between 0.7 to 0.9).

Canopy Fuels

Semivariance values are highly variable across each of the sites for CBD as show by the scatter of the points used to build the model (Figure 14). Most sites had excellent model fits (NM, LF, TF), but the CF pine savanna site had a poor fit with widely scattered semivariances. Exponential models were used for the three Montana sites, but the lack of distance-semivariance relationships for TF, CF, and SM required using a spherical, Gaussian, and pure nugget model, respectively (Table 13).

The characteristics of spatial variograms for the three canopy fuel characteristics seemed remarkably similar across sites (Table 13; Figure 15). For the semivariogram range, values ranged from 100 to 440 m for CBD, 310 to 600 m for CFL, and 230 to 407 m for CC. Lowest ranges were in the closed forests of LF and TF (lodgepole), while the highest values were for the open SM and CF forests. CFL had the highest patch sizes (450 to 600 m), and these were significantly different from CBD and CC (Figure 15). The sill and nugget were significantly different across the three canopy characteristics, with CBD consistently having the lower semivariance and CC with the highest (Figure 15), probably due to differences in how each are estimated. Moran's I statistics were also quite low for the canopy fuel characteristics with the highest value at 0.17 in the TF lodgepole pine site indicating a lack of spatial structure in canopy characteristics (Table 13). In general, Moran's I was highest on the TF and SM sites, with values around 0.1, and lowest on the CF pine savanna, with values less than 0.08, for all three canopy fuel characteristics. Moran's I values, however, were statistically similar across the three canopy characteristics with CC having the greatest variation in spatial structure (Figure 15).

It appears that canopy fuel characteristics are somewhat related to the inherent patch sizes (semivariogram range) of larger woody fuel (Figure 16). Large woody fuel ranges appeared to increase as canopy fuel increases in loading, bulk density, and cover, yet there seemed to be no relationship between canopy characteristics and litter+duff, shrubs, and fine woody debris ranges. It is odd that herb variogram ranges seemed to increase with canopy material, but this may be explained by the

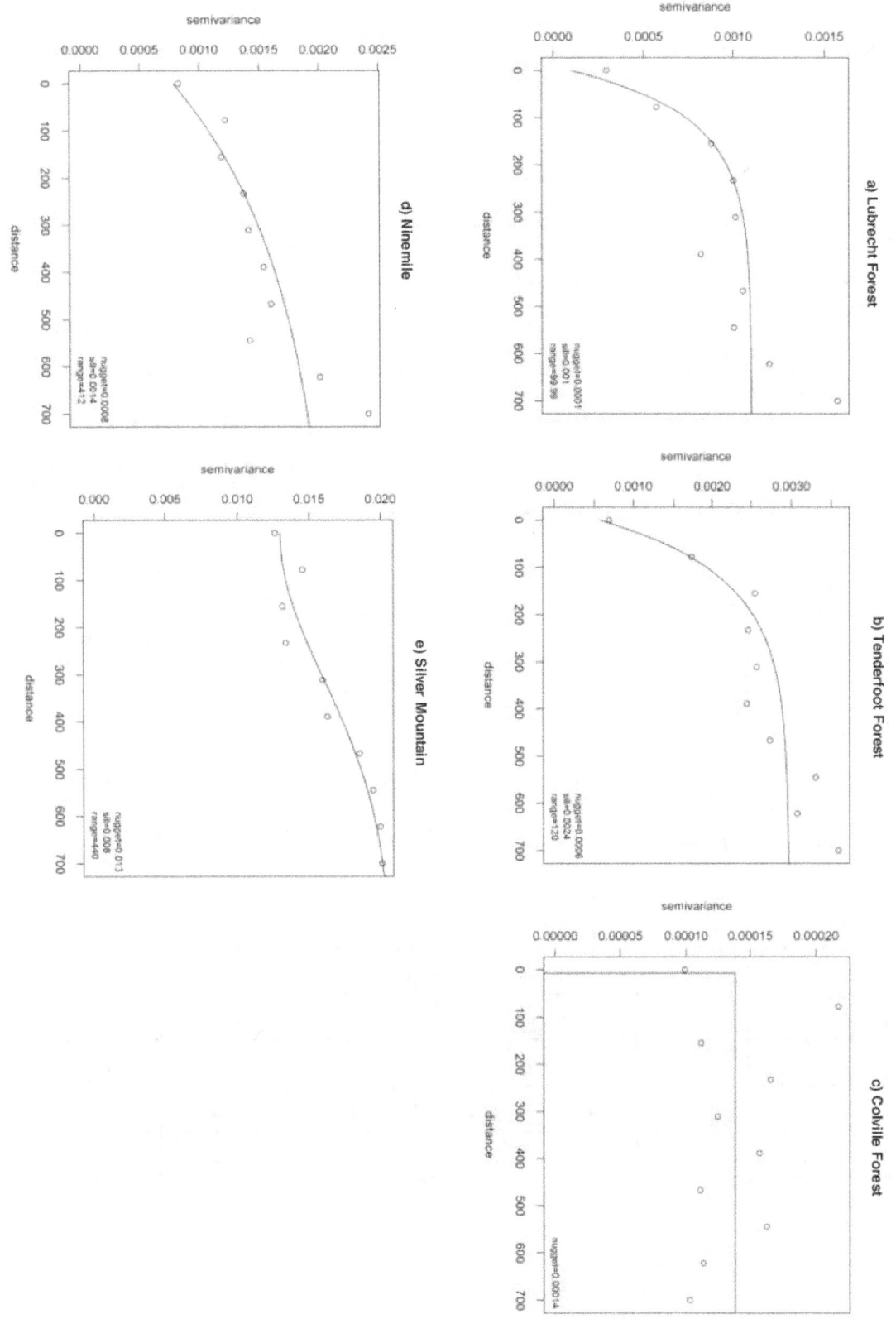

Figure 14. Semivariograms for canopy bulk density across all sites in the study (a) Lubrecht Forest, (b) Tenderfoot Forest, (c) Colville Forest, (d) Ninemile, and (e) Silver Mountain.

Table 13. Spatial semivariogram statistics for the three canopy fuel characteristics across the six sample sites. Model indicates the type of model used to fit the semivariogram.

Statistic	Bighole Valley (BV) Sagebrush Grass[a]	Silver Mountain (SM) Pinyon-Juniper	Colville Forest (CF) Pine Savannah	Ninemile (NM) Pine-Fir	Lubrecht Forest (LF) Pine-Fir-Larch	Tenderfoot Forest (TF) Lodgepole Pine
Canopy Bulk Density (CBD, kg m^{-3})						
Model[b]	-	gaussian	pure nugget	exponential	exponential	exponential
Range (m)	-	440	-	412	100	120
Sill	-	0.008	-	0.0014	0.001	0.0024
Nugget	-	0.013	0.00014	0.0008	0.0001	0.0006
Moran's I	-	*0.118	*0.083	*0.102	*0.045	0.0919
Geary's C		*0.861	1.065	*0.778	*0.721	*0.732
Canopy Fuel Loading (CFL, kg m^{-2})						
Model[2]	-	gaussian	pure nugget	exponential	exponential	spherical
Range	-	560	-	600	310	560
Sill	-	0.0497	-	0.020	0.0172	0.0102
Nugget	-	0.0501	0.0056	0.026	0.0154	0.0062
Moran's I	-	*0.146	*0.058	*0.092	*0.052	*0.174
Geary's C		*0.814	1.033	0.892	*0.805	*0.782
Canopy Cover (CC, percent)						
Model[2]	-	gaussian	pure nugget	pure nugget	exponential	gaussian
Range	-	407	-	-	230	300
Sill	-	0.159	-	-	0.048	0.0302
Nugget	-	0.202	0.107	0.1197	0.103	0.0266
Moran's I	-	*0.122	*0.069	*0.034	0.027	*0.162
Geary's C		*0.789	0.963	0.989	0.807	0.812

[a]No tree canopy existed on the Bighole Valley site.

[b]No existent anisotropy was examined.

*Indicates statistic is significant at $p < 0.01$.

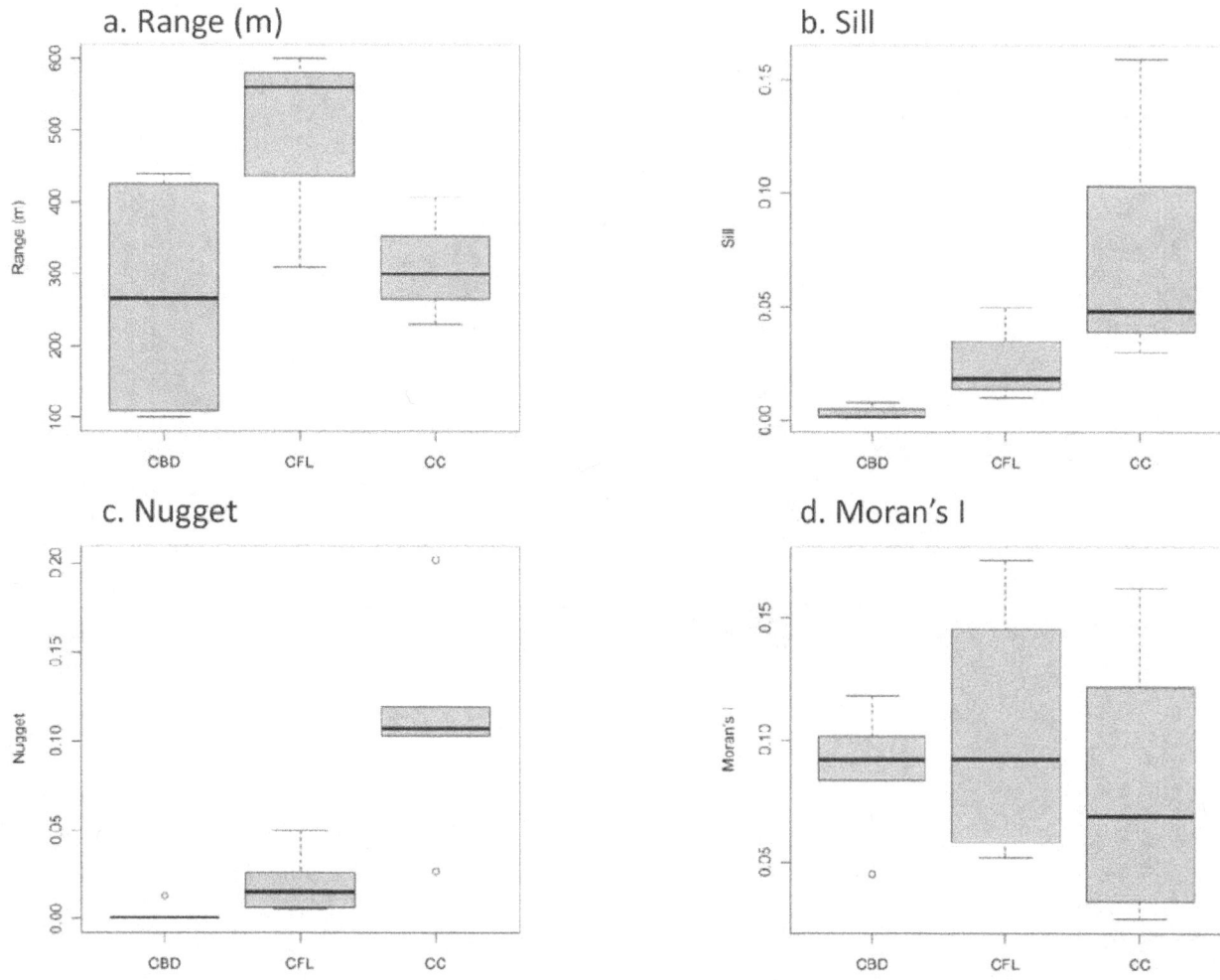

Figure 15. Box and whisker plots of the four spatial statistics (a) range, (b) sill, (c) nugget, and (d) Moran's I for the three canopy fuel components: canopy bulk density (CBD, kg m^{-3}); canopy fuel loading (CFL, kg m^{-2}); canopy cover (CC, %).

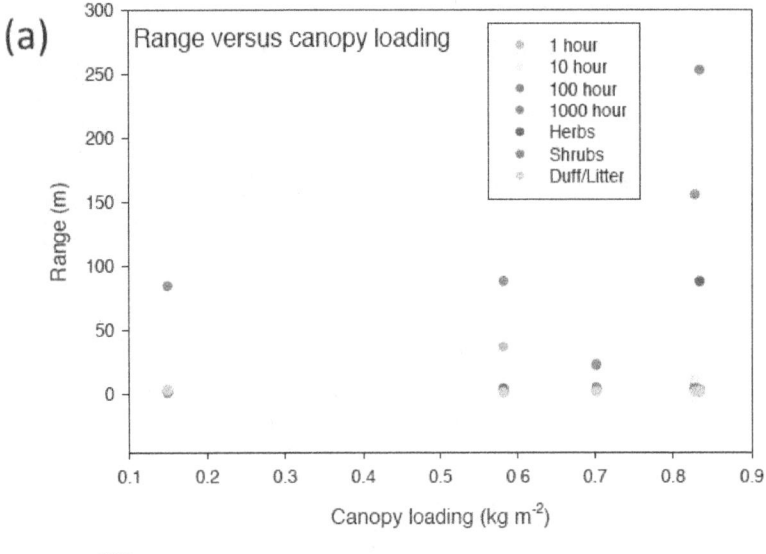

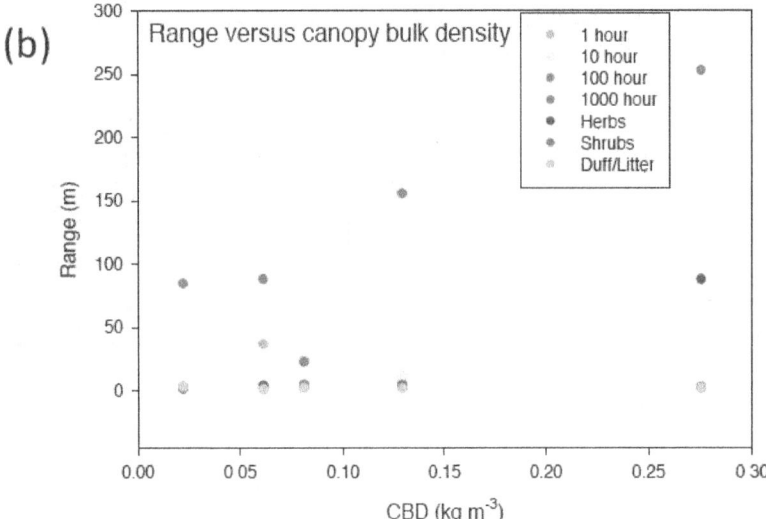

Figure 16. Semivariogram range statistics for loading of each surface fuel component by the average canopy fuel characteristics computed across all plots on all sites.

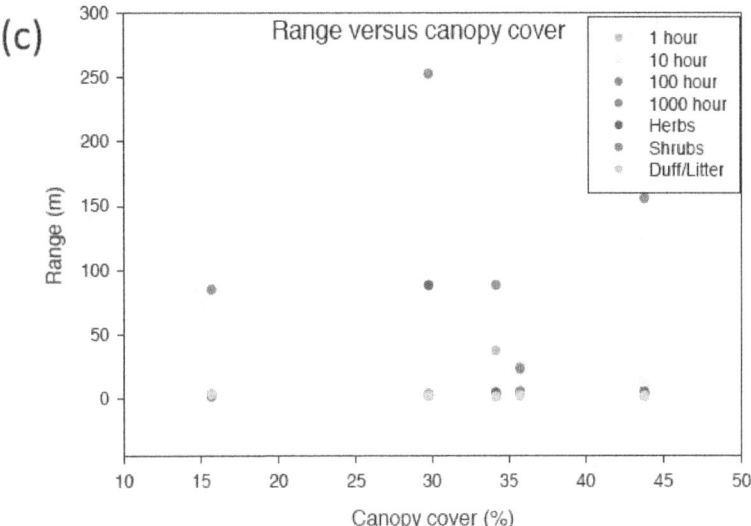

patchiness of herb coverage. CBD seemed to have the best fit with log loading semivariogram range.

Discussion

Perhaps the most important characteristic about wildland fuel is not its loading but the variability of that loading across the landscape, and this variability occurs at multiple scales depending on the size and type of fuel. The great heterogeneity of the fuel loading within small areas has more of an effect on fire behavior than the average loading (Parsons and others 2010) because fine-to-coarse scale spatial fuel distributions may influence fire spread and intensity more than the actual amount of that fuel. Moreover, the impact of this highly variable spread and intensity on the biophysical environment leaves behind a complex mosaic of fire effects that is governed not only by the scale of the fuel variability but also by the scale of the fire. Understanding this variability is the key to predicting complex, interacting fire behavior and effects.

Several important results from this study provide insight into understanding general fuel variability. First, and most obvious, is that all fuels are highly variable (Tables 7, 9). Most surface fuel components have properties that are highly variable: loading, for example, had variabilities that are often more than twice the mean, and we confined sampling to homogeneous stands. Second, it appears that this variability increases with fuel particle size; larger surface fuel properties are more variable than finer fuel properties (Table 7). Canopy fuel properties, on the other hand, have significantly lower variabilities than surface fuel components (less than 100 percent of mean), and this variability appears to be consistent across all canopy fuel characteristics (Table 9). It also appears that surface fuel loadings are not correlated to canopy fuel variables, general stand characteristics, and other surface fuel components (Table 11), but all canopy fuel variables were correlated to some commonly used stand characteristics (Table 10). Last, it appears that fuel loadings are rarely normally distributed with skewness statistics often greater than 1.0 for many components and sites (Table 7). These results are not new, nor are they unexpected, and they somewhat agree with results from other studies (Brown and Bevins 1986; Delisle and others 1988; Thaxton and Platt 2006; King and others 2008).

The findings of this study that are new concern the spatial distribution of this variability across the surface and canopy fuel components. It appears that surface fuel components vary across different spatial scales with finer fuels of litter, duff, herbs, shrubs, and fine woody fuels varying at scales of meters to tens of meters, and larger surface fuels, such as 100 and 1000 hr fuels, vary at scales of tens to hundreds of meters (Table 12). Canopy fuels vary at still coarser scales (100 to 400 m) (Table 13). Moreover, this spatial variability differs across sites, with closed canopy sites having somewhat smaller patch sizes than open canopies and rangeland settings (i.e., fuel component variability is highly variable across ecosystems). Larger fuels have less spatial structure than fine fuels as indicated by the low values of Moran's I (less than 0.2; Table 12), and spatial distribution of logs are somewhat related to canopy fuels (Figure 15). This difference in scale and spatial distribution across surface fuel components could partly explain the lack of correlation of most surface fuels to canopy fuel variables and stand characteristics even though the forest canopy is the source for most of the litter that falls on the surface fuelbed.

So, why are wildland fuels so variable? We feel that this variability is a result of many factors acting across different time and space scales. Most importantly, the sources of fuels, namely the plants, are often distributed across space in clumps or heterogeneous patches (Pukkala and Kolstrom 1991; Pacala and Deutschman 1995; Rochefort and Peterson 1996). Large fuels, such as large branches and tree boles, tend to accumulate directly under the plant sources, especially trees, but small fuels, such as needles and twigs, can be blown away from the plant by wind, creating a more homogeneous distribution (Harmon and others 1986). Smaller fuels decompose quickly, which may influence spatial variability, while large fuels decompose slowly over decades and tend to accumulate directly under plants, thereby increasing variability across space (Keane 2008a). However, it is the impact of disturbances, such as windthrow, wildland fires, and insect outbreaks, and their patterns, that are probably the most important factor that influences spatial fuel distributions (Brown and Bevins 1986). In mixed species stands, for example, fuels can unevenly accumulate underneath the dead individuals killed by mountain pine beetle (Page and Jenkins 2007; Jenkins and others 2008). Fires can kill and injure plants and consume fuels in a patchwork of burned and unburned areas that will subsequently influence the colonization of future plants over long time periods (King and others 2008).

One interesting dilemma resulting from this study is that if this spatial variability is so important in describing fuels, then why have the current fuel inputs to fire models continued to satisfy fire managers and researchers? None of the fire models account for the large variability in fuel characteristics, yet predictions from these models are used extensively in fire management with acceptable results. This could be because the one major factor influencing fire behavior and effects during large fire events is weather, not fuel, and weather might drive fire behavior predictions under severe drought, high temperatures, strong wind, and steep slope conditions (Bessie and Johnson 1995). Another reason may be that all fire behavior and effects models used in management are one-dimensional point models that are designed to be used for small, homogeneous areas on the landscape, and the high extrapolation error of point estimates across space may overwhelm the variability of fuel characteristics. These one-dimensional fire behavior and effects models may not have sufficient resolution to recognize subtle changes in fuel properties across space. It could also be that the fuel information is often calibrated or adjusted to compute values that match observed fire behavior (Burgan and Rothermel 1984), and this calibration has accounted for both loading and its variability. After all, fuels information in the fire behavior fuel models created by Anderson (1982) and Scott and Burgan (2005) are actually abstract representations of perceived fire behavior. Still, another reason might be that the high uncertainty in fuel sampling and fire behavior measurements make it difficult to actually validate the fire behavior and effects predictions. One thing is certain, if fire managers and researchers want more accurate and consistent estimates of fire at multiple scales, future fire models must account for fuel variability to comprehensively simulate fire behavior and effects (Thaxton and Platt 2006; Parsons and others 2010).

Study Findings

There are many aspects of our study results that need additional explanation to fully understand the findings. Our measured surface fuel loadings were consistent with those found in the literature, indicating that these sites had typical fuelbeds for northern Rocky Mountain sites (Brown and Bevins 1986). Moreover, the canopy fuel characteristics calculated in this study compared well with those studies that destructively measured canopy fuels (Scott and Reinhardt 2005; Reinhardt and others 2006), except for the SM pinyon-juniper site, which had a very high CFL and CBD because of the overestimation of canopy biomass using the allometric equations implemented in FUELCALC (Reinhardt and others 2006).

The high particle densities measured for the 1 and 10 hr downed woody fuels were comparable to values found in the literature. Our fine woody particle densities ranged from 482 to 657 kg m^{-3} with large ranges and variations (Table 7). In the most comprehensive compilation of fine woody particle densities, Harmon and others (2008) reported values ranging from approximately 400 to 650 kg m^{-3} for similar tree species encountered in this study. Nalder and others (1999) measured 430 to 620 kg m^{-3} for fine fuels in the boreal forests of western and northern Canada, and Nalder and others (1997) measured 493 to 607 kg m^{-3} for spruce fine fuels in the boreal forests of Alberta and Northwest Territories. Sackett (1980) measured particle densities of southwestern tree species and found they ranged from 390 to 635 kg m^{-3}, while Van Wagtendonk and others (1996) measured densities of 530 to 670 kg m^{-3} for Sierra Nevada conifers, and Ryan and Pickford (1978) measured mixed conifer fine wood densities of 340 to 620 kg m^{-3} in the Blue Mountains of Oregon and Washington. Interestingly, the ranges and variation of fine woody particle densities reported from these studies compares well with the variations calculated in our study.

The variability and mean of particle densities of the large woody fuels measured in this study also compared well with those measured in other studies. We found particle densities of 100 and 1000 hr size classes for downed woody ranged from 178 to 522 kg m^{-3} with lower variation than fine woody debris (Table 7). Harmon and others (2008) compiled ranges of approximately 200 to over 600 kg m^{-3}, and Green and others (1999) measured ranges of 300 to 550 kg m^{-3} for the same species encountered in our study. Our low coarse woody debris bulk densities are due to the high number of rotten logs found on our study sites, especially on the treated sites where rotten snags had fallen from thinning activities. The high particle densities measured at the SM site for pinyon-juniper downed wood seem consistent with values measured in Harmon and others (2008).

Most puzzling, however, were our measurements for bulk densities of the duff and litter layers (66 to 416 kg m^{-3} for CF and LF, respectively). They were much higher than the L-layer (only litter) bulk densities measured by Brown (1981), which ranged from 21 to 51 kg m^{-3}, higher than those measured by Snell (1979), which ranged from 23 to 32 kg m^{-3}, and higher than those measured by Brown (1970b), which ranged from 5 to 43 kg m^{-3} for xeric habitat types similar to those found in this study (these studies measured mostly the litter layer). However, our values tended to agree with the high bulk densities measured by Stephens and others (2004), which ranged from 54 to over 300 kg m^{-3} for California Sierra mixed conifer stands. Our values are high because of the presence of woody material and mineral soil within the litter+duff layer, especially on sites that had been thinned or grazed (LF, SM). Many woody fuel particles were embedded in the litter+duff layer and we decided to include these woody sticks in the computation of litter+duff bulk density even though these heavy woody particles substantially increased litter+duff bulk density on many plots. In fact, our high values compared well with the bulk densities of masticated fuel beds found by Kane and others (2009), which were 46 to 141 kg m^{-3} with high variability. We thought it was appropriate to include these woody particles since woody fuel particles must be above the duff layer to be sampled using standard methods (Lutes and others 2006). Our litter+duff profiles also had substantial amounts of mineral soil mixed with duff based on the high estimations of mineral content (greater than 40 percent on three sites).

The high magnitude and variability of the measured mineral contents of woody and litter+duff components were a result of a number of factors. The high litter+duff mineral contents (22 to 47 percent) were probably from the mixing of mineral soil into the litter+duff layer by soil fauna, freeze-thaw cycles, grazing, and management activities (fuel treatments). We also found it difficult to identify the duff-mineral soil interface on many plots, so some mineral soil could have been mixed with the litter+duff sample profile during collection. Our values somewhat agree with Hood and Wu (2006) who found duff mineral contents were approximately 32 percent in Jeffrey pine-white fir forests and 42 percent in pine-oak woodlands. We believe that the reason 1 hr woody fuels had higher mineral contents than the larger woody fuels was because mineral soil residue on fine woody fuels contributed more to the overall particle weight than the mineral soil on larger fuel particles, probably explaining why our fine woody fuel particle densities were much higher than those presented in the literature. Ragland and others (1991) found clean wood mineral contents ranged from 0.1 to 0.6 percent, which agrees with our findings for 1000 hr logs. But our fine woody fuels ranged from 1 to 8 percent, which is an order of magnitude more than clean wood. This could be from mineral soil residue on the fine woody material, or it could be from the bark on some of these small particles because bark mineral contents can range from 3 to 5 percent (Ragland and others 1991). Default values for mineral contents in fire behavior fuel models are set at 5.5 percent across all woody size classes (Burgan and Rothermel 1984; Scott and Burgan 2005), yet we found great variation in mineral contents across sites and components (Table 7), which can have great implications for the simulation of fire behavior because high mineral contents dampen fire behavior.

Study Limitations

This study has some limitations that may have influenced the results. First, out of logistical necessity, we sampled the woody fuel in the size classes commonly used by fire behavior models, which may be major source of variation in the study results (Table 1). Loadings in the 100 hr fuels, for example, can be highly variable because particle diameters range from 2.5 cm to 8 cm, resulting in a near ten-fold range in volume or loading. To further compound this problem, branch size distributions differ by species and position in the canopy. Subalpine fir, for example, has smaller branches than ponderosa pine (Minore 1979; Reinhardt and others 2006) and, as a result, there is little chance that fir branches can be big enough to represent the entire range of 100 hr fuel. This problem has haunted wildland fuel science and management for some time because size class variability isn't fully represented in fuel models, sampling methods, or fuel maps. In results from this study that are reported elsewhere, we explored using the distribution of loading across fuel particle sizes as a means to correct conventional fuel loading estimates and to develop new sampling methods (Keane and others 2012). Smoke emissions predictions, carbon inventories, and fuel consumption would be improved if fuels were sampled at size classes that are appropriate for the resolution of the sampling method and the ecology of downed woody debris (Harmon and others 1986). For example, size classes could be based on volume, the resolution of newly developed sampling methods, or variability of particle or component density. We are trying to develop a method that uses a fuel size-loading distribution relationship to calculate loading from particle counts in fixed area plots.

Another concern is the low nanoplot, microplot, and subplot sampling densities at small scales. Due to logistical and cost constraints, there were only four intensive microplot grids (4 x 25 m^2 = 100 m^2) in the 1 km^2 sample grid. This 1 percent sample could be too small for accurate descriptions of spatial variability of surface fuels at fine scales. The distance between subplots for log loadings may have also been too great to accurately describe log spatial variability. However, extensive statistical analysis of our data revealed that the subplot size was large enough to minimize log fuel sampling variability, but we could have had more intensive sampling at 5-, 10-, and 15-m distances for fine woody fuels and logs.

Plot sizes used in this study may have been inappropriate for some fuel components. For logistical reasons, we only used four sampling frames for describing fuels, when in reality, the surface fuelbed may have components that are not effectively sampled at these scales. Large branches (100 hr), for example, may be more appropriately sampled with a 10 m^2 microplot because of their rarity within a stand and because the estimated inherent patch size was 1 to 5 m (Table 12). This is somewhat evident in the high spatial variogram nugget values (Table 12). The high measurement error could be a result of inappropriate sample frames or ineffective measurement techniques (photoload adjustments). However, the ranges of many of the surface and canopy fuel properties appeared to compare well with our sampling design: (1) macroplot size of 400 m^2 matched with 80 to 400 m canopy fuel patch size, (2) subplot size of 100 m^2 matched with the 22 to 200 m patch sizes, and (3) microplots (1 m^2) matched with shrub, herb, 1 hr, and 10 hr woody patch sizes (0.5 to 2 m). Those that didn't match were the 100 hr microplots that had a 1 to 3.6 m patch size, and nanoplots (0.25 m^2) that had litter+duff patch sizes of 0.5 to 8 m (Table 12)

This study was only implemented on six study sites that represented a small number of forest and range vegetation types in the northern Rocky Mountains. As a result, these study results are probably only specific to the few sites that we sampled. It took well over a month to conduct the measurements on one study site, so our sampling time was limited because of cost concerns. Moreover, it was difficult to find study sites that fit our selection criteria because the complex interactions among wildland fire, management activities, and topography rarely created the large, flat, homogeneous sites needed for this study. In the future, we will relax site selection criteria and move from small homogeneous 1 km^2 patches to entire landscapes such as the Tenderfoot Creek Experimental Forest (Figure 5).

We feel that the somewhat higher particle densities measured in this study are primarily a result of the inaccurate measurement of particle volume using the water displacement method to estimate volume (Fasth and others 2010). While this method is better than calculating volume using diameter and length measurements, it tends to under-estimate volume, which results in over-estimations of particle densities because the mass of the particle is divided by the volume. Small wood particles tend to absorb water in small cracks and fissures, causing less displacement and resulting displacement values are so low that small errors in volume estimates result in large errors in the calculation of density. These twigs weigh so little and have such low volumes that minor measurement errors of 0.1 cm^3 can cause large changes in particle density. A 6 g twig, for example, that displaces 0.5 cm^3 of water would have a density of approximately 120 kg m^{-3}, but if the displacement is 0.4 cm^3, the density would be 150 kg m^{-3}, over 25 percent higher. Another reason particle densities were high was because of the residual mineral soil present on some of the sticks. We decided to leave this mineral soil on the particles because it is more representative of its condition in the fuelbed.

Our decision to sample the duff and litter as one component was also a major limitation of the study. We found that it is difficult to consistently and accurately differentiate between the duff and litter fuel both in the field and in the office because the organic soil profile is more a gradient of decomposed material rather than a set of two distinctly different fuel components. This profile is constantly being mixed by animals, disturbance, and soil micro- and macro-fauna, making it difficult to find the subtle seam between litter and duff (Harmon and others 1986). Rather than introducing the additional uncertainty of litter-duff differentiation, we decided to group litter and duff together. Unfortunately, most fire behavior and effects models require separate litter and duff inputs (Reinhardt and Keane 1998), and most of the values found in the literature are separated by litter and duff (Brown 1970b, 1981; Snell 1979).

Last, the estimation of canopy fuel characteristics has some major limitations. Both CFL and CBD were indirectly estimated using the allometric canopy fuel equations contained in FUELCALC, and while most of our tree species in the study were represented in FUELCALC, equations for the species on the SM site (pinyon pine and juniper) were missing and substituted with other equations from similar species. This resulted in an overestimation of canopy fuel because the clumpy nature of pinyon-juniper trees was not properly represented in FUELCALC. Moreover, the visual estimation of CC was done using 10 percent cover classes (5 to 15 percent, 15 to 25 percent, for example), and this also increased variation of this canopy variable.

Research and Management Implications

The findings from this study may have great implications to fire management and research that could fundamentally change the way we describe fuels and model fire in the future. Most importantly, it is clear that wildland fuel components vary greatly across different scales. This means that fuel sampling and mapping must accommodate the inherent scales of each fuel component. Counting intersects of all sizes of woody fuels crossing a sampling plane, for example, may ineffectively characterize fuel loadings, and similarly, using satellite imagery with only one resolution may not accommodate the accurate estimation of fuel loadings across all components. Future field methods must integrate scale into the sampling design, such as using nested fixed area sampling techniques designed to fit fuel particle patch sizes, to improve accuracies. Fine fuels, for example, should be sampled with a frame that is large enough to minimize spatial sampling bias (1 to 2 m^2). Hierarchically nested fixed-area plot designs, similar to the one used in this study, may be needed where fine fuels are sampled within 1 to 2 m^2 microplots, logs are sampled on 50 to 100 m^2 plots, and canopy fuels are sampled on 400 to 1000 m^2 plots. Critical research is needed to develop methods that efficiently quantify fuels within fixed plots and are also easy for management to use with minimal training and resources.

Quantification of wildland fuel loadings is often accomplished using standard fuel sampling protocols that are greatly dependent on woody fuel particle densities and shrub, herb, and litter+duff bulk densities (Brown and others 1982). Particle and bulk densities are used extensively in field sampling methods to estimate loading (Lutes and others 2006). The great variability that we found in these density measurements (Table 7) across both sites and fuel components suggests that estimating fuel loadings is even more difficult than previously thought since most fuel sampling methods use an average wood density value to calculate loadings for all woody components (Brown 1970a, 1974). Results from this study show that not only are wood densities different across components; they are also highly variable within a component (Table 7; Figure 10). This complicates an already complex procedure for sampling fuels in that it now appears that wood density must also be assessed at the sample site to get accurate loading estimates. Innovative techniques are needed to quickly assess particle densities to accurately estimate fuel loadings. The same is true with field sampling litter+duff, shrub, and herbaceous loadings. Our bulk density values were highly variable and site specific, so new methods are needed to adjust bulk densities for local situations to accurately compute loadings from depth measurements. Photographs, for example, can be taken of shrub, herb, and litter+duff fuelbeds with measured bulk densities, and field people can select the picture that best matches the fuelbed conditions (Keane and Dickinson 2007a, 2007b; Ottmar and Vihnanek 2000).

Fuel maps are now essential tools for predicting fire spread and intensity (Reeves and others 2006), but few of these maps incorporate scale and variability of fuel components in their design (Keane and others 2001). Variability of fine fuels within the 30-m pixel size commonly used in land management may be so great that it will overwhelm fuel quantification, compromise accuracy assessments, and ineffectively predict fire behavior and effects. Fine scale variations in fuel loadings and structure can also affect fire spread and subsequent fire intensity (Parsons and others 2010). There are at least two alternatives for spatially describing fuel components at their inherent scale. First, the resolution of imagery, modeling, and GIS analysis should match the appropriate resolution of the fuel component being mapped; twigs, for example, should be mapped using 1 to 5 m pixel imagery. Second, the fire behavior and effects models that use fuel maps could internally intensify the mapping grid with algorithms that stochastically distribute fuels across space at the appropriate resolutions. While this spatial stochastic modeling approach would not create the actual fuelbed for that pixel, it would create a fuelbed with the same variability and distributional characteristics. We created maps that distributed fuels at their appropriate scale and variability based on the spatial statistics computed in this study to show how future fuel maps can be developed (Figure 17).

Fuel classifications, such as fire behavior fuel models (Scott and Burgan 2005), fuel loading models (Lutes and others 2009), or fuel characteristics classification system (Ottmar and others 2007), may be inappropriate for future fire behavior and effects applications because they lack a description of fuel variability across space. These classifications are "point" estimations of fuel loadings, yet many mapping efforts assign categories from these classifications to entire areas, such as stands, polygons, or landscapes, ignoring the influence of the high fuel variability on fire prediction. The assignment of one classification category to a polygon discounts the fact that fuel components vary across different scales within that polygon and that they are highly variable across space. Moreover, most mapping efforts assign fuel classification categories to the categories of other vegetation classifications (Keane and others 1999), yet this study found that surface fuel components are rarely correlated to each other or to stand and canopy characteristics (Table 11) and that the variability of the vegetation, as described by canopy fuel variables, is rarely at the same scale as the surface fuel (Figure 16). We are conducting research in the possible development of the next generation of fuel models that contain the statistical properties of the spatial distribution of fuel components so that effective fuel maps can be developed at any scale and resolution (Figure 17).

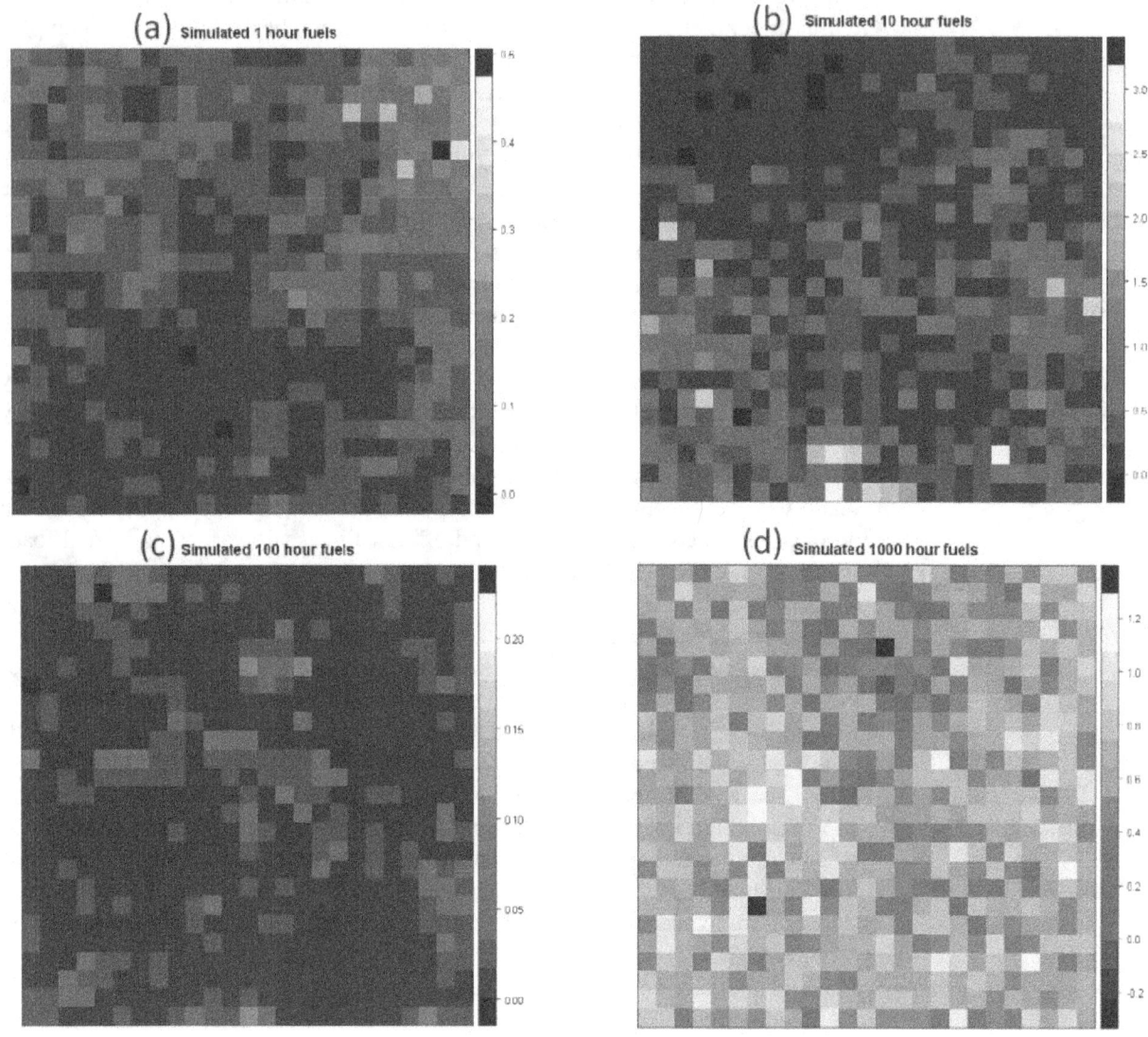

Figure 17. An example of maps of the four down dead woody fuel components created using statistical stochastic algorithms parameterized from findings of this study.

Summary and Conclusions

It comes as no surprise to anyone who works in wildland fuel science and management that the properties and characteristics of fuels are highly variable. Most things in nature are highly variable to ensure their continued existence. Fuels, however, seem to take variability to another level, especially in a spatial and temporal context. Not only do wildland fuels have a variability that exceeds twice the mean within small areas, but this variability is distributed across space at unique scales for each fuel component with smaller fuels having smaller inherent patch sizes of 1 to 10 m than large fuels which are distributed in 100 to 500 m patch sizes. And these inherent patch sizes for each fuel component can change across different sites, becoming larger in forests with discontinuous canopies, for example. Moreover, it appears surface fuel loadings are rarely normally distributed, rendering parametric statistics inappropriate for many fuel analyses, and surface fuel loadings are poorly correlated with any canopy fuel or stand-level characteristic, which means that stand and vegetation characteristics may not be useful for mapping surface fuels, but they may be useful for canopy fuel characteristics.

These findings further complicate the process of describing and quantifying fuels for fire management and research. It appears that designing accurate, one-size-fits-all sampling, classification, and mapping approach for describing wildland fuels will be difficult because of high spatial variability. Each component must be sampled at its own scale to reduce a large amount of variation introduced because the resolution of the sampling approach did not match the scale of the data. And the high variation in fuel properties, such as particle density, may preclude cost-effective, generalized approaches at quantifying fuel loadings. If the particle density varies by a factor of two within an individual particle, then estimating accurate fuel loadings may require complex and costly sampling methods for determining particle density, which may be impractical for fire management.

Fire management and research may want to take a different approach for describing fuel characteristics, such as loading, in the future. Instead of using the central tendency statistics, such as the mean, median, or mode, to describe fuels in an area, future wildland fuel analyses should account for the high spatial variation by using novel statistical approaches, such as stochastic modeling of fuel loading probability distributions, to capture the full impact of fuel variability in space. This also means that point-level fire behavior and effects modeling probably will not improve in accuracy without explicit representation of spatial distributions even though these models are constantly refined and modified to include additional detail in combustion simulation because spatial fuel variability will overwhelm minor changes in model design. Future fire models will need a three-dimensional implementation to fully account for fuel variability in their simulations.

References

Agee, J. K., B. Bahro, M. A. Finney, P. N. Omi, D. B. Sapsis, C. N. Skinner, J. W. van Wagtendonk, and C. W. Weatherspoon. 2000. The use of shaded fuelbreaks in landscape fire management. Forest Ecology and Management 127:55-66.

Agee, J. K. and M. H. Huff. 1987. Fuel succession in a western hemlock/Douglas-fir forest. Canadian Journal of Forest Research 17:697-704.

Agee, J. K. and C. N. Skinner. 2005. Basic principles of forest fuel reduction treatments. Forest Ecology and Management 211:83-96.

Agee, J. K., C. S. Wright, N. Williamson, and M. H. Huff. 2002. Foliar moisture content of Pacific Northwest vegetation and its relation to wildland fire behavior. Forest Ecology and Management 167:57-66.

Albini, F. A. 1976. Estimating wildfire behavior and effects. General Technical Report INT-30, USDA Forest Service, Intermountain Research Station, Ogden, UT.

Albini, F. A. 1999. Crown fire spread rate modeling. Progress Report RJVA RMRS-99525, Fire Sciences Laboratory P.O. Box 8089, Missoula, MT, USA.

Alexander, M. E. 1988. Help with making crown fire hazard assessments. Pages 147-153 *in* Protecting people and homes from wildfire in the Interior West: Proceedings of the symposium and workshop. USDA Forest Service.

Anderson, H. E. 1982. Aids to determining fuel models for estimating fire behavior. General Technical Report INT-122, USDA Forest Service, Intermountain Research Station, Ogden, UT, USA.

Anderson, H. E. 1990. Predicting equilibrium moisture content of some foliar forest litter in the northern Rocky Mountains. Research Paper INT-429, USDA Forest Service, Intermountain Research Station, Ogden, UT, USA.

Andrews, P. L. 2008. BehavePlus fire modeling system, version 4.0: Variables. General Technical Report RMRS-GTR-213WWW, USDA Forest Service, Rocky Mountain Research Station, Fort Collins, CO.

Augustine, D. 2010. Spatial versus temporal variation in precipitation in a semiarid ecosystem. Landscape Ecology 25:913-925.

Bate, L. J., T. R. Torgersen, M. J. Wisdom, and E. O. Garton. 2004. Performance of sampling methods to estimate log characteristics for wildlife. Forest Ecology and Management 199:83-102.

Bellehumeur, C. and P. Legendre. 1998. Multiscale sources of variation in ecological variables: modeling spatial dispersion, elaborating sampling designs. Landscape Ecology 13:15-25.

Bessie, W. C. and E. A. Johnson. 1995. The relative importance of fuels and weather on fire behaviour in subalpine forests. Ecology 76:747-762.

Brais, S., F. Sadi, Y. Bergeron, and Y. Grenier. 2005. Coarse woody debris dynamics in a post-fire jack pine chronosequence and its relation with site productivity. Forest Ecology and Management 220:216-226.

Brown, J. K. 1970a. A method for inventorying downed woody fuel. General Technical Report INT-16, USDA Forest Service, Intermountain Research Station, Ogden, UT.

Brown, J. K. 1970b. Physical fuel properties of ponderosa pine forest floors and cheatgrass. Research Paper INT-74, USDA Forest Service, Intermountain Forest and Range Experiment Station, Ogden, UT.

Brown, J. K. 1974. Handbook for inventorying downed woody material. General Technical Report GTR-INT-16, USDA Forest Service, Intermountain Forest and Range Experiment Station, Ogden, UT, USA.

Brown, J. K. 1978. Weight and density of crowns of Rocky Mountain conifers. Research Paper INT-197, USDA Forest Service Intermountain Forest and Range Experiment Station, Ogden, UT, USA.

Brown, J. K. 1981. Bulk densities of nonuniform surface fuels and their application to fire modeling. Forest Science 27:667-683.

Brown, J. K. and C. D. Bevins. 1986. Surface fuel loadings and predicted fire behavior for vegetation types in the northern Rocky Mountains. Research Note INT-358, USDA Forest Service, Intermountain Forest and Range Experiment Station, Ogden, UT, USA.

Brown, J. K., R. D. Oberheu, and C. M. Johnston. 1982. Handbook for inventoring surface fuels and biomass in the Interior West. General Technical Report INT-129, USDA Forest Service, Intermountain Forest and Range Experiment Station, Ogden, UT, USA.

Brown, J. K. and T. E. See. 1981. Downed dead woody fuel and biomass in the northern Rocky Mountains. Gen. Tech. Rep. INT-117, USDA Forest Service, Intermountain Forest and Range Experiment Station, Ogden, UT, USA.

Burgan, R. E. and R. C. Rothermal. 1984. BEHAVE: fire behavior prediction and fuel modeling system—FUEL subsystem. General Technical Report INT-167, USDA Forest Service.

Call, P. T. and F. A. Albini. 1997. Aerial and surface fuel consumption in crown fires. International Journal of Wildland Fire 7:259-264.

Cary, G. J., R. E. Keane, R. H. Gardner, S. Lavorel, M. D. Flannigan, I. D. Davies, C. Li, J. M. Lenihan, T. S. Rupp, and F. Mouillot. 2006. Comparison of the sensitivity of landscape-fire-succession models to variation in terrain, fuel pattern and climate. Landscape Ecology 21:121-137.

Chen, Z., K. Grady, S. Stephens, J. Villa-Castillo, and M. R. Wagner. 2006. Fuel reduction treatment and wildfire influence on carabid and tenebrionid community assemblages in the ponderosa pine forest of northern Arizona, USA. Forest Ecology and Management 225:168-177.

Cliff, A. D., and K. Ord. 1970. Spatial autocorrelation: A review of existing and new measures with applications. Economic Geography 46:269-292.

Cressie, A. G. 1985. Fitting variogram models using weighted least squares. Journal of the International Association of Mathematical Geology 17:563-586.

Cruz, M. G., M. E. Alexander, and R. H. Wakimoto. 2003. Assessing canopy fuel stratum characteristics in crown fire prone fuel types of western North America. International Journal of Wildland Fire 12:39-50.

DeBano, L. F., D. G. Neary, and P. F. Ffolliott. 1998. Fire's Effect on Ecosystems. John Wiley and Sons, New York, USA.

Deeming, J. E., R. E. Burgan, and J. D. Cohen. 1977. The National Fire Danger Rating System—1978. General Technical Report INT-39, USDA Forest Service, Intermountain Forest and Range Experiment Station, Ogden, UT.

Delisle, G. P., P. M. Woodard, S. J. Titus, and A. F. Johnson. 1988. Sample size and variability of fuel weight estimates in natural stands of lodgepole pine. University of Alberta Department of Forest Science, Edmonton, Alberta, Canada.

Fasth, B., M. E. Harmon, C. W. Woodall, and J. Sexton. 2010. Evaluation of techniques for determining the density of fine woody debris. Research Paper NRS-11, USDA Forest Service, Northern Research Station, Newton Square, PA.

Finkral, A. J. and A. M. Evans. 2008. The effects of a thinning treatment on carbon stocks in a northern Arizona ponderosa pine forest. Forest Ecology and Management 255:2743-2750.

Finney, M. A. 1998a. FARSITE: Fire ARea Simulator—model development and evaluation. Research Paper RMRS-RP-4. USDA Forest Service, Rocky Mountain Research Station, Fort Collins, CO.

Finney, M. A. 1998b. Relationships between landscape fuel patterns and fire growth. Working draft.

Fortin, M.-J. 1999. Spatial statistics in landscape ecology. Pages 253-279 in J. M. Klopatek and R. H. Gardner, editors. Landscape ecological analysis: issues and applications. Springer-Verlag, Inc., New York, USA.

Fosberg, M. A. 1970. Drying rates of heartwood below fiber saturation. Forest Science 16:57-63.

Gary, H. L. 1976. Crown structure and distribution of biomass in a lodgepole pine stand. Research Paper RM-165, USDA Forest Service, Rocky Mountain Forest and Range Experiment Station.

Graham, R. T., S. McCaffrey, and T. B. Jain. 2004. Science basis for changing forest structure to modify wildfire behavior and severity. General Technical Report RMRS-GTR-120, USDA Forest Service, Rocky Mountain Research Station, Fort Collins, CO.

Green, D. W., J. E. Winandy, and K. D. E. 1999. Mechanical Properties of Wood. Pages 4.1-4.45 *in* Wood handbook: Wood as an engineering material. USDA Forest Service, Forest Products Laboratory, Madison, WI.

Grunwald, S., K. R. Reddy, J. P. Prenger, and M. M. Fisher. 2007. Modeling of the spatial variability of biogeochemical soil properties in a freshwater ecosystem. Ecological Modelling 201:521-535.

Habeeb, R. L., J. Trebilco, S. Wotherspoon, and C. R. Johnson. 2005. Determining natural scales of ecological systems. Ecological Monographs 75:467-487.

Hagan, J. M. and S. L. Grove. 1999. Coarse woody debris. Journal of Forestry January: 6-11.

Hardy, C. C., R.E. Burgan, and R. D. Ottmar. 1999. A database for spatial assessments of fire characteristics, fuel profiles, and PM10 emissions. Journal of Sustainable Forestry.

Harmon, M. E., J. F. Franklin, F. J. Swanson, P. Sollins, S. V. Gregory, J. D. Lattin, N. H. Anderson, S. P. Cline, N. G. Aumen, J. R. Sedell, G. W. Lienkaemper, K. Cromack, and K. W. Cummins. 1986. Ecology of coarse woody debris in temperate ecosystems. Advances in Ecological Research. 15:133-302.

Harmon, M. E., C. W. Woodall, B. Fasth, and J. Sexton. 2008. Woody detritus density and density reduction factors for tree species in the United States: A synthesis. General Technical Report NRS-29, USDA Forest Service, Northern Research Station, Newton Square, PA.

Hartford, R. A. 1990. Smoldering combustion limits in peat as influenced by moisture, mineral content, and organic bulk density. Pages 282-286 *in* Proceedings of the 10th conference on fire and forest meterology. Forestry Canada, Petawawa National Forestry Institute, Chalk River, Ontario, Canada.

Hiers, J. K., J. J. O'Brien, R. J. Mitchell, J. M. Grego, and E. L. Loudermilk. 2009. The wildland fuel cell concept: an approach to characterize fine-scale variation in fuels and fire in frequently burned longleaf pine forests. International Journal of Wildland Fire 18:315-325.

Hood, S. and R. Wu. 2006. Estimating fuel bed loadings in masticated areas. Pages 333-345 *in* Fuels management—How to measure success. Proceedings, RMRS-P-41, USDA Forest Service, Rocky Mountain Research Station, Fort Collins, CO, USA.

Ingalsbee, T. 2005. Fire ecology: Issues, management, policy, and opinions. Fire Ecology 1:85-99.

Isaaks, E. H. and R. M. Srivastava. 1989. Applied Geostatistics. Oxford University Press, New York, USA.

Jenkins, M. A., E. Hebertson, W. Page, and C. A. Jorgensen. 2008. Bark beetles, fuels, fire and implications for forest management in the Intermountain West. Forest Ecology and Management 254:16-34.

Jia, G. J., I. C. Burke, A. F. H. Goetz, M. R. Kaufmann, and B. C. Kindel. 2006. Assessing spatial patterns of forest fuel using AVIRIS data. Remote Sensing of Environment 102:318-327.

Kalabokidis, K. and P. Omi. 1992. Quadrat analysis of wildland fuel spatial variability. International Journal of Wildland Fire 2:145-152.

Kane, J. M., J. M. Varner, and E. E. Knapp. 2009. Novel fuel characteristics associated with mechanical mastication treatments in northern California and south-western Oregon, USA. International Journal of Wildland Fire 18:686-697.

Keane, R. E. 2008a. Surface fuel litterfall and decomposition in the northern Rocky Mountains, U.S.A. Research Paper, RMRS-RP-70, USDA Forest Service, Rocky Mountain Research Station, Fort Collins, CO.

Keane, R. E. 2008b. Surface fuel litterfall and decomposition in the northern Rocky Mountains, USA. Research Paper RMRS-RP-70, USDA Forest Service, Rocky Mountain Research Station, Fort Collins, Colorado.

Keane, R. E., R. E. Burgan, and J. V. Wagtendonk. 2001. Mapping wildland fuels for fire management across multiple scales: Integrating remote sensing, GIS, and biophysical modeling. International Journal of Wildland Fire 10:301-319.

Keane, R. E. and L. J. Dickinson. 2007a. Development and evaluation of the photoload sampling technique. Research Paper RMRS-RP-61CD, USDA Forest Service, Rocky Mountain Research Station, Fort Collins, CO.

Keane, R. E. and L. J. Dickinson. 2007b. The Photoload sampling technique: estimating surface fuel loadings using downward looking photographs. General Technical Report RMRS-GTR-190, USDA Forest Service, Rocky Mountain Research Station, Fort Collins, CO.

Keane, R. E., T. L. Frescino, M. C. Reeves, and J. Long. 2006. Mapping wildland fuels across large regions for the LANDFIRE prototype project. Pages 367-396 in The LANDFIRE prototype project: Nationally consistent and locally relevant geospatial data for wildland fire management. General Technical Report RMRS-GTR-175, USDA Forest Service, Rocky Mountain Research Station, Fort Collins, CO.

Keane, R. E., D. G. Long, K. M. Schmidt, S. A. Mincemoyer, and J. L. Garner. 1998. Mapping fuels for spatial fire simulations using remote sensing and biophysical modeling. Pages 301-316 in Natural resource management using remote sensing and GIS: Proceedings of the Seventh Forest Service Remote Sensing Applications Conference, Nassau Bay, Texas, April 6-10, 1998. Bethesda, MD, American Society for Photogrammetry and Remote Sensing.

Kennedy, R., T. Spies, and M. Gregory. 2008. Relationships of dead wood patterns with biophysical characteristics and ownership according to scale in Coastal Oregon, USA. Landscape Ecology 23:55-68.

King, K. J., R. A. Bradstock, G. J. Cary, J. Chapman, and J. B. Marsden-Smedley. 2008. The relative importance of fine-scale fuel mosaics on reducing fire risk in south-west Tasmania, Australia. International Journal of Wildland Fire 17:421-430.

Linn, R. R. 1997. A transport model for prediction of wildfire behavior. Dissertation. New Mexico State University, Las Cruces, USA.

Lutes, D. C., R. E. Keane, and J. F. Caratti. 2009. A surface fuels classification for estimating fire effects. International Journal of Wildland Fire 18:802-814.

Lutes, D. C., R. E. Keane, J. F. Caratti, C. H. Key, N. C. Benson, S. Sutherland, and L. J. Gangi. 2006. FIREMON: Fire effects monitoring and inventory system. General Technical Report RMRS-GTR-164-CD, USDA Forest Service, Rocky Mountain Research Station, Fort Collins, CO, USA.

Maglione, D. S. and A. M. Diblasi. 2004. Exploring a valid model for the variogram of an isotropic spatial process. Stochastic Environmental Research and Risk Assessment 18:366-376.

McBratney, A. G. and A. G. Webster. 1986. Choosing functions for semi-variograms and fitting them to sampling estimates. Journal of Soil Science 37:617-639.

McCollum, J. M. 2005. Grid-based sampling designs and area estimation. In Seventh Annual Forest Inventory and Analysis Symposium, Ogden, UT.

Miller, C. and D. L. Urban. 2000. Connectivity of forest fuels and surface fire regimes. Landscape Ecology 15:145-154.

Minore, D. 1979. Comparative autecological characteristics of northwestern tree species: a literature review. General Technical Report PNW-87, USDA Forest Service, Pacific Northwest Forest and Range Experiment Station, Portland, OR, USA.

Moran, P. A. P. 1950. Notes on continuous stochastic phenomenon. Biometrika 37:17-23.

Nalder, I. A., R. W. Wein, M. E. Alexander, and W. J. De Groot. 1997. Physical properties of dead and downed round-wood fuels in the boreal forests of Alberta and Northwest Territories. Canadian Journal of Forest Research 27:1513-1517.

Nalder, I. A., R. W. Wein, M. E. Alexander, and W. J. d. Groot. 1999. Physical properties of dead and downed round-wood fuels in the boreal forests of western and northern Canada. International Journal of Wildland Fire 9:85-99.

Ohlson, D. W., T. M. Berry, R. W. Gray, B. A. Blackwell, and B. C. Hawks. 2006. Multi-attribute evaluation of landscape-level fuel management to reduce wildfire risk. Forest Policy and Economics 8:824-837.

Okafor, Fabian C. and H. Lee. 2000. Double sampling for ratio and regression estimation with subsampling the nonrespondents. Survey Methodology 26:183-188.

Ottmar, R. D. 1983. Predicting fuel consumption by fire stages to reduce smoke from slash fires. Pages 87-106 in Proceedings from the Annual Meeting, Northwest Forest Fire Council. USDA Forest Service, Olympia, WA.

Ottmar, R. D., M.F. Burns, J.N. Hall, and A. D. Hanson. 1993. CONSUME users guide. General Technical Report PNW-GTR-304, USDA Forest Service, Pacific Northwest Research Station, Portland, OR.

Ottmar, R. D., D. V. Sandberg, C. L. Riccardi, and S. J. Prichard. 2007. An overview of the Fuel Characteristic Classification System—Quantifying, classifying, and creating fuelbeds for resource planning. Canadian Journal of Forest Research 37:2383-2393.

Ottmar, R. D. and R. E. Vihnanek. 2000. Stereo photo series for quantifying natural fuels. Volume VI: Longleaf pine, pocosin, and marshgrass types in the southeast United States. PMS-835, National Wildfire Coordinating Group National Interagency Fire Center, Boise, ID.

Pacala, S. W. and D. H. Deutschman. 1995. Details that matter: The spatial distribution of individual trees maintains forest ecosystem function. Oikos 74:357-365.

Page, W. and M. J. Jenkins. 2007. Mountain pine beetle-induced changes to selected lodgepole pine fuel complexes within the Intermountain Region. Forest Science 53:507-520.

Parsons, R. A., W. E. Mell, and P. McCauley. 2010. Linking 3D spatial models of fuels and fire: Effects of spatial heterogeneity on fire behavior. Ecological Modelling 222:679-691.

Peters, D. P. C., I. Mariotto, K. M. Havstad, and L. W. Murray. 2006. Spatial variation in remnant grasses after a grassland-to-shrubland state change: implications for restoration. Rangeland Ecology and Management 59:343-350.

Powell, S. and A. Hansen. 2007. Conifer cover increase in the greater Yellowstone ecosystem: Frequency, rates, and spatial variation. Ecosystems 10:204-216.

Pukkala, T. and T. Kolstrom. 1991. Effect of spatial pattern of trees on the growth of a Norway spruce stand: A simulation model. Silva Fennica 25:117-131.

Ragland, K. W., D. J. Aerts, and A. J. Baker. 1991. Properties of wood for combustion analysis. Bioresource Technology 37:161-168.

Reeves, M. C., J. R. Kost, and K. C. Ryan. 2006. Fuels products of the LANDFIRE project. Pages 239-249 in Fuels management—How to measure success. Proceedings RMRS-P-41, USDA Forest Service, Rocky Mountain Research Station, Portland, OR.

Reich, R. M., J. E. Lundquist, and V. A. Bravo. 2004. Spatial models for estimating fuel loads in the Black Hills, South Dakota, USA. International Journal of Wildland Fire 13:119-129.

Reinhardt, E. and N. L. Crookston. 2003. The fire and fuels extension to the Forest Vegetation Simulator. General Technical Report RMRS-GTR-116, USDA Forest Service, Rocky Mountain Research Station, Fort Collins, CO.

Reinhardt, E. and L. Holsinger. 2010. Effects of fuel treatments on carbon-disturbance relationships in forests of the northern Rocky Mountains. Forest Ecology and Management 259:1427-1435.

Reinhardt, E. and R. E. Keane. 1998. FOFEM—A First Order Fire Effects Model. Fire Management Notes 58:25-28.

Reinhardt, E., J. H. Scott, K. L. Gray, and R. E. Keane. 2006. Estimating canopy fuel characteristics in five conifer stands in the western United States using tree and stand measurements. Canadian Journal Forest Research 36:1-12.

Reinhardt, E. D., R. E. Keane, D. E. Caulkin, and J. D. Cohen. 2008. Objectives and considerations for wildland fuel treatment in forested ecosystems of the interior western United States. Forest Ecology and Management 256:1997-2006.

Ribeiro Jr., P. J. and P. J. Diggle. 2001. geoR: A package for geostatistical analysis. R-NEWS 1.

Roberts, S. D. and J. N. Long. 1992. Production efficiency of Abies lasiocarpa: Influence of vertical distribution of leaf area. Canadian Journal of Forest Research 22: 1230-1234

Rocca, M. E. 2009. Fine-scale patchiness in fuel load can influence initial post-fire understory composition in a mixed conifer forest, Sequoia National Park, California. Natural Areas Journal 29:126-132.

Rochefort, R. M. and D. L. Peterson. 1996. Temporal and spatial distribution of trees in subalpine meadows of Mount Rainier National Park, Washington, U.S.A. Arctic and Alpine Research. 28:52-59.

Rodeghiero, M. and A. Cescatti. 2008. Spatial variability and optimal sampling strategy of soil respiration. Forest Ecology and Management 255:106-112.

Rollins, M. G., R. E. Keane, and R. Parsons. 2004. Mapping ecological attributes using gradient analysis and remote sensing. Ecological Applications 14:75-95.

Rothermel, R. C. 1972. A mathematical model for predicting fire spread in wildland fuels. Research Paper INT-115, USDA Forest Service, Intermountain Forest and Range Experiment Station, Ogden, UT.

Rothermel, R. C. 1991. Predicting behavior and size of crown fires in the Northern Rocky Mountains. Research Paper INT-438, USDA Forest Service, Intermountain Forest and Range Experiment Station, Ogden, UT, USA.

Russo, D. and M. Bouton. 1992. Statistical analysis of spatial variability in unsaturated flow parameters. Water Resources Review 28:1911-1925.

Ryan, K. C. and S. G. Pickford. 1978. Physical properties of woody fuels in the Blue Mountains of Oregon and Washington. PNW-315, USDA Forest Service, Pacific Northwest Forest and Range Experiment Station.

Sackett, S. S. 1980. Woody fuel particle size and specific gravity of Southwestern tree species. Colorado State University, Fort Collins, CO.

Sandberg, D. V., R. D. Ottmar, and G. H. Cushon. 2001. Characterizing fuels in the 21st century. International Journal of Wildland Fire 10:381-387.

Sando, R. W. and C. H. Wick. 1972. A method of evaluating crown fuels in forest stands. Research Paper NC-84, USDA Forest Service, North Central Forest Experiment Station, Saint Paul, MN, USA.

Scott, J. and R. E. Burgan. 2005. A new set of standard fire behavior fuel models for use with Rothermel's surface fire spread model. General Technical Report RMRS-GTR-153, USDA Forest Service, Rocky Mountain Research Station, Fort Collins, CO.

Scott, J. H. 1999. NEXUS: A system for assessing crown fire hazard. Fire Management Notes 59:21-24.

Scott, J. H. and E. D. Reinhardt. 2005. Stereo photo guide for estimating canopy fuel characteristics in conifer stands. General Technical Report RMRS-GTR-145, USDA Forest Service, Rocky Mountain Research Station, Fort Collins, CO.

Sikkink, P. and R. E. Keane. 2008. A comparison of five sampling techniques to estimate surface fuel loading in montane forests. International Journal of Wildland Fire 17:363-379.

Snell, J. A. K. 1979. Direct estimation of surface fuel bulk density and loading in western Montana and northern Idaho. Thesis, University of Montana, Missoula.

Sokal, R. R. and F. J. Rohlf. 1981. Biometry. W.H. Freeman and Company, San Francisco, CA, USA.

Stephens, S. L., M. Finney, and H. Schentz. 2004. Bulk density and fuel loads of ponderosa pine and white fir forest floors: Impacts of leaf morphology. Northwest Science 78:93-104.

Thaxton, J. M. and W. J. Platt. 2006. Small-scale fuel variation alters fire intensity and shrub abundance in a pine savanna. Ecology 87:1331-1337.

Thorhallsdottir, T. E. 1990. The dynamics of a grassland community: a simultaneous investigation of spatial and temporal heterogeneity at various scales. Journal of Ecology 78:884-908.

Townsend, D. E. and S. D. Fuhlendorf. 2010. Evaluating relationships between spatial heterogeneity and the biotic and abiotic environments. The American Midland Naturalist 163:351-365.

van Wagner, C. E. 1977. Conditions for the start and spread of crown fire. Canadian Journal of Forest Research 7:23-34.

Van Wagtendonk, J. W., J. M. Benedict, and W. M. Sydoriak. 1996. Physical properties of woody fuel particles of Sierra Nevada conifers. International Journal of Wildland Fire 6:117-123.

Van Wagtendonk, J. W., W. M. Sydoriak, and J. M. Benedict. 1998. Heat content variation of Sierra Nevada conifers. International Journal of Wildland Fire 8:147-158.

Woodall, C. W. and L. M. Nagel. 2006. Coarse woody type: A new method for analyzing coarse woody debris and forest change. Forest Ecology and Management 227:115-121.

Woodard, P. M. and R. E. Martin. 1980. Duff weight and depth in a high elevation Pinus contorta Dougl. forest. Canadian Journal of Forest Research 10:7-9.